William Shakespeare (bapt. 26 April 1564 – 23 April 1616) was an English poet, playwright and actor, widely regarded as the greatest writer in the English language and the world's greatest dramatist. He is often called England's national poet and the "Bard of Avon". His extant works, including collaborations, consist of approximately 39 plays, 154 sonnets, two long narrative poems, and a few other verses, some of uncertain authorship. His plays have been translated into every major living language and are performed more often than those of any other playwright. Shakespeare was born and raised in Stratford-upon-Avon, Warwickshire. At the age of 18, he married Anne Hathaway, with whom he had three children: Susanna and twins Hamnet and Judith. Sometime between 1585 and 1592, he began a successful career in London as an actor, writer, and part-owner of a playing company called the Lord Chamberlain's Men, later known as the King's Men. At age 49 (around 1613), he appears to have retired to Stratford, where he died three years later. (Source: Wikipedia)

Literary works:
The Tempest
The Two Gentlemen of Verona
The Merry Wives of Windsor
Measure for Measure
The Comedy of Errors
Much Ado About Nothing
Love's Labour's Lost
A Midsummer Night's Dream
The Merchant of Venice
As You Like It
The Taming of the Shrew
All's Well That Ends Well
Twelfth Night
The Winter's Tale
Pericles, Prince of Tyre
The Two Noble Kinsmen

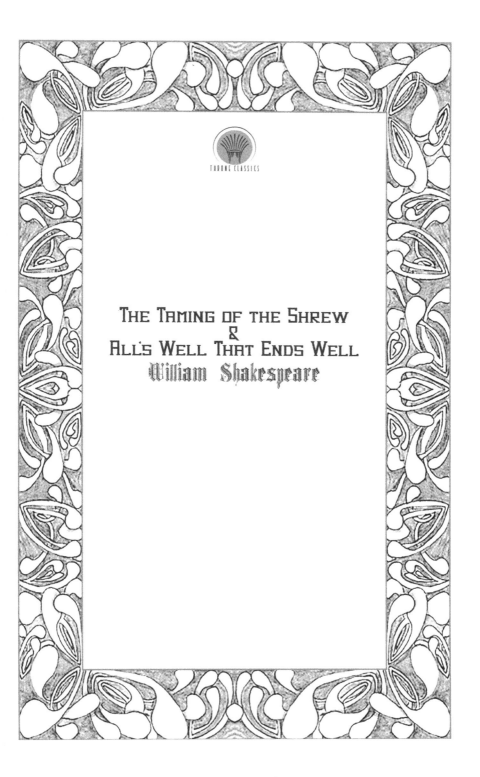

THRONE CLASSICS

The Taming of the Shrew
&
All's Well That Ends Well
William Shakespeare

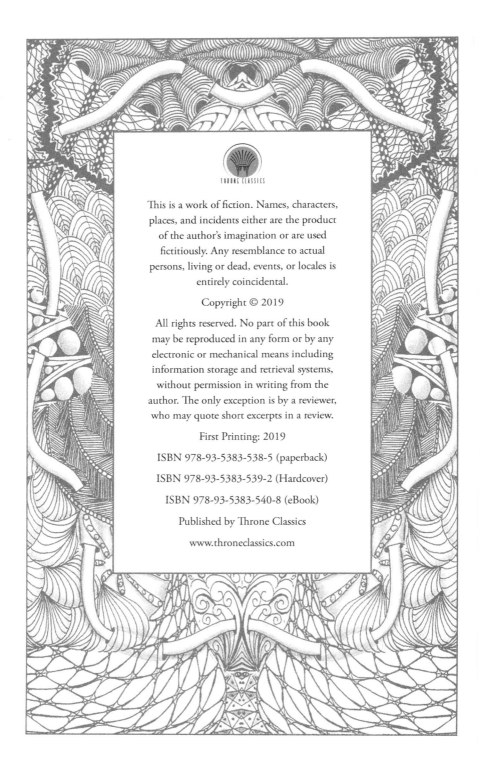

Copyright © 2019

First Printing: 2019

ISBN 978-93-5383-538-5 (paperback)

ISBN 978-93-5383-539-2 (Hardcover)

ISBN 978-93-5383-540-8 (eBook)

Published by Throne Classics

www.throneclassics.com

Contents

The Taming of the Shrew
&
All's Well That Ends Well

THE TAMING OF THE SHREW

Dramatis Personæ

Persons in the Induction

A LORD

CHRISTOPHER SLY, a tinker

HOSTESS

PAGE

PLAYERS

HUNTSMEN

SERVANTS

BAPTISTA MINOLA, a rich gentleman of Padua

VINCENTIO, an old gentleman of Pisa

LUCENTIO, son to Vincentio; in love with Bianca

PETRUCHIO, a gentleman of Verona; suitor to Katherina

Suitors to Bianca

GREMIO

HORTENSIO

Servants to Lucentio

TRANIO

BIONDELLO

Servants to Petruchio

GRUMIO

CURTIS

PEDANT, set up to personate Vincentio

Daughters to Baptista

KATHERINA, the shrew

BIANCA

WIDOW

Tailor, Haberdasher, and Servants attending on Baptista and Petruchio

SCENE: Sometimes in Padua, and sometimes in PETRUCHIO'S house in the country.

INDUCTION

SCENE I. Before an alehouse on a heath.

Enter Hostess and Sly

SLY.

I'll pheeze you, in faith.

HOSTESS.

A pair of stocks, you rogue!

SLY.

Y'are a baggage; the Slys are no rogues; look in the chronicles: we came in with Richard Conqueror. Therefore, paucas pallabris; let the world slide. Sessa!

HOSTESS.

You will not pay for the glasses you have burst?

SLY.

No, not a denier. Go by, Saint Jeronimy, go to thy cold bed and warm thee.

HOSTESS.

I know my remedy; I must go fetch the third-borough.

[Exit]

SLY.

Third, or fourth, or fifth borough, I'll answer him by law. I'll not budge an inch, boy: let him come, and kindly.

[Lies down on the ground, and falls asleep.]

Horns winded. Enter a Lord from hunting, with Huntsmen and Servants.

LORD.

Huntsman, I charge thee, tender well my hounds;

Brach Merriman, the poor cur is emboss'd,

And couple Clowder with the deep-mouth'd brach.

Saw'st thou not, boy, how Silver made it good

At the hedge-corner, in the coldest fault?

I would not lose the dog for twenty pound.

FIRST HUNTSMAN.

Why, Bellman is as good as he, my lord;

He cried upon it at the merest loss,

And twice today pick'd out the dullest scent;

Trust me, I take him for the better dog.

LORD.

Thou art a fool: if Echo were as fleet,

I would esteem him worth a dozen such.

But sup them well, and look unto them all;

Tomorrow I intend to hunt again.

FIRST HUNTSMAN.

I will, my lord.

LORD.

[Sees Sly.] What's here? One dead, or drunk?

See, doth he breathe?

SECOND HUNTSMAN.

He breathes, my lord. Were he not warm'd with ale,

This were a bed but cold to sleep so soundly.

LORD.

O monstrous beast! how like a swine he lies!

Grim death, how foul and loathsome is thine image!

Sirs, I will practise on this drunken man.

What think you, if he were convey'd to bed,

Wrapp'd in sweet clothes, rings put upon his fingers,

A most delicious banquet by his bed,

And brave attendants near him when he wakes,

Would not the beggar then forget himself?

FIRST HUNTSMAN.

Believe me, lord, I think he cannot choose.

SECOND HUNTSMAN.

It would seem strange unto him when he wak'd.

LORD.

Even as a flattering dream or worthless fancy.

Then take him up, and manage well the jest.

Carry him gently to my fairest chamber,

And hang it round with all my wanton pictures;

Balm his foul head in warm distilled waters,

And burn sweet wood to make the lodging sweet.

Procure me music ready when he wakes,

To make a dulcet and a heavenly sound;

And if he chance to speak, be ready straight,

And with a low submissive reverence

Say 'What is it your honour will command?'

Let one attend him with a silver basin

Full of rose-water and bestrew'd with flowers;

Another bear the ewer, the third a diaper,

And say 'Will't please your lordship cool your hands?'

Someone be ready with a costly suit,

And ask him what apparel he will wear;

Another tell him of his hounds and horse,

And that his lady mourns at his disease.

Persuade him that he hath been lunatic;

And, when he says he is—say that he dreams,

For he is nothing but a mighty lord.

This do, and do it kindly, gentle sirs;

It will be pastime passing excellent,

If it be husbanded with modesty.

FIRST HUNTSMAN.

My lord, I warrant you we will play our part,

As he shall think by our true diligence,

He is no less than what we say he is.

LORD.

Take him up gently, and to bed with him,

And each one to his office when he wakes.

[Sly is bourne out. A trumpet sounds.]

Sirrah, go see what trumpet 'tis that sounds:

[Exit Servant.]

Belike some noble gentleman that means,

Travelling some journey, to repose him here.

Re-enter Servant.

How now! who is it?

SERVANT.

An it please your honour, players

That offer service to your lordship.

LORD.

Bid them come near.

Enter Players.

Now, fellows, you are welcome.

PLAYERS.

We thank your honour.

LORD.

Do you intend to stay with me tonight?

PLAYER.

So please your lordship to accept our duty.

LORD.

With all my heart. This fellow I remember

Since once he play'd a farmer's eldest son;

'Twas where you woo'd the gentlewoman so well.

I have forgot your name; but, sure, that part

Was aptly fitted and naturally perform'd.

PLAYER.

I think 'twas Soto that your honour means.

LORD.

'Tis very true; thou didst it excellent.

Well, you are come to me in happy time,

The rather for I have some sport in hand

Wherein your cunning can assist me much.

There is a lord will hear you play tonight;

But I am doubtful of your modesties,

Lest, over-eying of his odd behaviour,—

For yet his honour never heard a play,—

You break into some merry passion

And so offend him; for I tell you, sirs,

If you should smile, he grows impatient.

PLAYER.

Fear not, my lord; we can contain ourselves,

Were he the veriest antick in the world.

LORD.

Go, sirrah, take them to the buttery,

And give them friendly welcome everyone:

Let them want nothing that my house affords.

[Exit one with the Players.]

Sirrah, go you to Barthol'mew my page,

And see him dress'd in all suits like a lady;

That done, conduct him to the drunkard's chamber,

And call him 'madam,' do him obeisance.

Tell him from me—as he will win my love,—

He bear himself with honourable action,

Such as he hath observ'd in noble ladies

Unto their lords, by them accomplished;

Such duty to the drunkard let him do,

With soft low tongue and lowly courtesy,

And say 'What is't your honour will command,

Wherein your lady and your humble wife

May show her duty and make known her love?'

And then with kind embracements, tempting kisses,

And with declining head into his bosom,

Bid him shed tears, as being overjoy'd

To see her noble lord restor'd to health,

Who for this seven years hath esteemed him

No better than a poor and loathsome beggar.

And if the boy have not a woman's gift

To rain a shower of commanded tears,

An onion will do well for such a shift,

Which, in a napkin being close convey'd,

Shall in despite enforce a watery eye.

See this dispatch'd with all the haste thou canst;

Anon I'll give thee more instructions.

[Exit Servant.]

I know the boy will well usurp the grace,

Voice, gait, and action of a gentlewoman;

I long to hear him call the drunkard husband;

And how my men will stay themselves from laughter

When they do homage to this simple peasant.

I'll in to counsel them; haply my presence

May well abate the over-merry spleen,

Which otherwise would grow into extremes.

[Exeunt.]

SCENE II. A bedchamber in the LORD'S house.

Sly is discovered in a rich nightgown, with Attendants: some with apparel, basin, ewer, and other appurtenances; and Lord, dressed like a servant.

SLY.

For God's sake! a pot of small ale.

FIRST SERVANT.

Will't please your lordship drink a cup of sack?

SECOND SERVANT.

Will't please your honour taste of these conserves?

THIRD SERVANT.

What raiment will your honour wear today?

SLY.

I am Christophero Sly; call not me honour nor lordship. I ne'er drank sack in my life; and if you give me any conserves, give me conserves of beef. Ne'er ask me what raiment I'll wear, for I have no more doublets than backs, no more stockings than legs, nor no more shoes than feet: nay, sometime more feet than shoes, or such shoes as my toes look through the over-leather.

LORD.

Heaven cease this idle humour in your honour!

O, that a mighty man of such descent,

Of such possessions, and so high esteem,

Should be infused with so foul a spirit!

SLY.

What! would you make me mad? Am not I Christopher Sly, old Sly's son of Burton-heath; by birth a pedlar, by education a cardmaker, by transmutation a bear-herd, and now by present profession a tinker? Ask Marian Hacket, the fat ale-wife of Wincot, if she know me not: if she say I am not fourteen pence on the score for sheer ale, score me up for the lyingest knave in Christendom. What! I am not bestraught. Here's—

THIRD SERVANT.

O! this it is that makes your lady mourn.

SECOND SERVANT.

O! this is it that makes your servants droop.

LORD.

Hence comes it that your kindred shuns your house,

As beaten hence by your strange lunacy.

O noble lord, bethink thee of thy birth,

Call home thy ancient thoughts from banishment,

And banish hence these abject lowly dreams.

Look how thy servants do attend on thee,

Each in his office ready at thy beck:

Wilt thou have music? Hark! Apollo plays,

[Music.]

And twenty caged nightingales do sing:

Or wilt thou sleep? We'll have thee to a couch

Softer and sweeter than the lustful bed

On purpose trimm'd up for Semiramis.

Say thou wilt walk: we will bestrew the ground:

Or wilt thou ride? Thy horses shall be trapp'd,

Their harness studded all with gold and pearl.

Dost thou love hawking? Thou hast hawks will soar

Above the morning lark: or wilt thou hunt?

Thy hounds shall make the welkin answer them

And fetch shrill echoes from the hollow earth.

FIRST SERVANT.

Say thou wilt course; thy greyhounds are as swift

As breathed stags; ay, fleeter than the roe.

SECOND SERVANT.

Dost thou love pictures? We will fetch thee straight

Adonis painted by a running brook,

And Cytherea all in sedges hid,

Which seem to move and wanton with her breath

Even as the waving sedges play with wind.

LORD.

We'll show thee Io as she was a maid

And how she was beguiled and surpris'd,

As lively painted as the deed was done.

THIRD SERVANT.

Or Daphne roaming through a thorny wood,

Scratching her legs, that one shall swear she bleeds

And at that sight shall sad Apollo weep,

So workmanly the blood and tears are drawn.

LORD.

Thou art a lord, and nothing but a lord:

Thou hast a lady far more beautiful

Than any woman in this waning age.

FIRST SERVANT.

And, till the tears that she hath shed for thee

Like envious floods o'er-run her lovely face,

She was the fairest creature in the world;

And yet she is inferior to none.

SLY.

Am I a lord? and have I such a lady?

Or do I dream? Or have I dream'd till now?

I do not sleep: I see, I hear, I speak;

I smell sweet savours, and I feel soft things:

Upon my life, I am a lord indeed;

And not a tinker, nor Christophero Sly.

Well, bring our lady hither to our sight;

And once again, a pot o' the smallest ale.

SECOND SERVANT.

Will't please your mightiness to wash your hands?

[Servants present a ewer, basin and napkin.]

O, how we joy to see your wit restor'd!

O, that once more you knew but what you are!

These fifteen years you have been in a dream,

Or, when you wak'd, so wak'd as if you slept.

SLY.

These fifteen years! by my fay, a goodly nap.

But did I never speak of all that time?

FIRST SERVANT.

O! yes, my lord, but very idle words;

For though you lay here in this goodly chamber,

Yet would you say ye were beaten out of door,

And rail upon the hostess of the house,

And say you would present her at the leet,

Because she brought stone jugs and no seal'd quarts.

Sometimes you would call out for Cicely Hacket.

SLY.

Ay, the woman's maid of the house.

THIRD SERVANT.

Why, sir, you know no house nor no such maid,

Nor no such men as you have reckon'd up,

As Stephen Sly, and old John Naps of Greece,

And Peter Turph, and Henry Pimpernell;

And twenty more such names and men as these,

Which never were, nor no man ever saw.

SLY.

Now, Lord be thanked for my good amends!

ALL.

Amen.

Enter the Page, as a lady, with Attendants.

SLY.

I thank thee; thou shalt not lose by it.

PAGE.

How fares my noble lord?

SLY.

Marry, I fare well; for here is cheer enough.

Where is my wife?

PAGE.

Here, noble lord: what is thy will with her?

SLY.

Are you my wife, and will not call me husband?

My men should call me lord: I am your goodman.

PAGE.

My husband and my lord, my lord and husband;

I am your wife in all obedience.

SLY.

I know it well. What must I call her?

LORD.

Madam.

SLY.

Alice madam, or Joan madam?

LORD.

Madam, and nothing else; so lords call ladies.

SLY.

Madam wife, they say that I have dream'd

And slept above some fifteen year or more.

PAGE.

Ay, and the time seems thirty unto me,

Being all this time abandon'd from your bed.

SLY.

'Tis much. Servants, leave me and her alone.

Madam, undress you, and come now to bed.

PAGE.

Thrice noble lord, let me entreat of you

To pardon me yet for a night or two;

Or, if not so, until the sun be set:

For your physicians have expressly charg'd,

In peril to incur your former malady,

That I should yet absent me from your bed:

I hope this reason stands for my excuse.

SLY.

Ay, it stands so that I may hardly tarry so long; but I would be loath to fall into my dreams again: I will therefore tarry in despite of the flesh and the blood.

Enter a Messenger.

MESSENGER.

Your honour's players, hearing your amendment,

Are come to play a pleasant comedy;

For so your doctors hold it very meet,

Seeing too much sadness hath congeal'd your blood,

And melancholy is the nurse of frenzy:

Therefore they thought it good you hear a play,

And frame your mind to mirth and merriment,

Which bars a thousand harms and lengthens life.

SLY.

Marry, I will; let them play it. Is not a commonty a Christmas gambold or a tumbling-trick?

PAGE.

No, my good lord; it is more pleasing stuff.

SLY.

What! household stuff?

PAGE.

It is a kind of history.

SLY.

Well, we'll see't. Come, madam wife, sit by my side and let the world slip: we shall ne'er be younger.

ACT I

SCENE I. Padua. A public place.

Flourish. Enter Lucentio and Tranio.

LUCENTIO.

Tranio, since for the great desire I had

To see fair Padua, nursery of arts,

I am arriv'd for fruitful Lombardy,

The pleasant garden of great Italy,

And by my father's love and leave am arm'd

With his good will and thy good company,

My trusty servant well approv'd in all,

Here let us breathe, and haply institute

A course of learning and ingenious studies.

Pisa, renowned for grave citizens,

Gave me my being and my father first,

A merchant of great traffic through the world,

Vincentio, come of the Bentivolii.

Vincentio's son, brought up in Florence,

It shall become to serve all hopes conceiv'd,

To deck his fortune with his virtuous deeds:

And therefore, Tranio, for the time I study,

Virtue and that part of philosophy

Will I apply that treats of happiness

By virtue specially to be achiev'd.

Tell me thy mind; for I have Pisa left

And am to Padua come as he that leaves

A shallow plash to plunge him in the deep,

And with satiety seeks to quench his thirst.

TRANIO.

Mi perdonato, gentle master mine;

I am in all affected as yourself;

Glad that you thus continue your resolve

To suck the sweets of sweet philosophy.

Only, good master, while we do admire

This virtue and this moral discipline,

Let's be no stoics nor no stocks, I pray;

Or so devote to Aristotle's checks

As Ovid be an outcast quite abjur'd.

Balk logic with acquaintance that you have,

And practise rhetoric in your common talk;

Music and poesy use to quicken you;

The mathematics and the metaphysics,

Fall to them as you find your stomach serves you:

No profit grows where is no pleasure ta'en;

In brief, sir, study what you most affect.

LUCENTIO.

Gramercies, Tranio, well dost thou advise.

If, Biondello, thou wert come ashore,

We could at once put us in readiness,

And take a lodging fit to entertain

Such friends as time in Padua shall beget.

But stay awhile; what company is this?

TRANIO.

Master, some show to welcome us to town.

[Lucentio and Tranio stand aside.]

Enter Baptista, Katherina, Bianca, Gremio and Hortensio.

BAPTISTA.

Gentlemen, importune me no farther,

For how I firmly am resolv'd you know;

That is, not to bestow my youngest daughter

Before I have a husband for the elder.

If either of you both love Katherina,

Because I know you well and love you well,

Leave shall you have to court her at your pleasure.

GREMIO.

To cart her rather: she's too rough for me.

There, there, Hortensio, will you any wife?

KATHERINA.

[To Baptista] I pray you, sir, is it your will

To make a stale of me amongst these mates?

HORTENSIO.

Mates, maid! How mean you that? No mates for you,

Unless you were of gentler, milder mould.

KATHERINA.

I' faith, sir, you shall never need to fear;

I wis it is not half way to her heart;

But if it were, doubt not her care should be

To comb your noddle with a three-legg'd stool,

And paint your face, and use you like a fool.

HORTENSIO.

From all such devils, good Lord deliver us!

GREMIO.

And me, too, good Lord!

TRANIO.

Husht, master! Here's some good pastime toward:

That wench is stark mad or wonderful froward.

LUCENTIO.

But in the other's silence do I see

Maid's mild behaviour and sobriety.

32

Peace, Tranio!

TRANIO.

Well said, master; mum! and gaze your fill.

BAPTISTA.

Gentlemen, that I may soon make good

What I have said,—Bianca, get you in:

And let it not displease thee, good Bianca,

For I will love thee ne'er the less, my girl.

KATHERINA.

A pretty peat! it is best put finger in the eye, and she knew why.

BIANCA.

Sister, content you in my discontent.

Sir, to your pleasure humbly I subscribe:

My books and instruments shall be my company,

On them to look, and practise by myself.

LUCENTIO.

Hark, Tranio! thou mayst hear Minerva speak.

HORTENSIO.

Signior Baptista, will you be so strange?

Sorry am I that our good will effects

Bianca's grief.

GREMIO.

Why will you mew her up,

Signior Baptista, for this fiend of hell,

And make her bear the penance of her tongue?

BAPTISTA.

Gentlemen, content ye; I am resolv'd.

Go in, Bianca.

[Exit Bianca.]

And for I know she taketh most delight

In music, instruments, and poetry,

Schoolmasters will I keep within my house

Fit to instruct her youth. If you, Hortensio,

Or, Signior Gremio, you, know any such,

Prefer them hither; for to cunning men

I will be very kind, and liberal

To mine own children in good bringing up;

And so, farewell. Katherina, you may stay;

For I have more to commune with Bianca.

[Exit.]

KATHERINA.

Why, and I trust I may go too, may I not? What! shall I be appointed hours, as though, belike, I knew not what to take and what to leave? Ha!

[Exit.]

GREMIO.

You may go to the devil's dam: your gifts are so good here's none will hold you. Their love is not so great, Hortensio, but we may blow our nails together, and fast it fairly out; our cake's dough on both sides. Farewell: yet,

34

for the love I bear my sweet Bianca, if I can by any means light on a fit man to teach her that wherein she delights, I will wish him to her father.

HORTENSIO.

So will I, Signior Gremio: but a word, I pray. Though the nature of our quarrel yet never brooked parle, know now, upon advice, it toucheth us both,—that we may yet again have access to our fair mistress, and be happy rivals in Bianca's love,—to labour and effect one thing specially.

GREMIO.

What's that, I pray?

HORTENSIO.

Marry, sir, to get a husband for her sister.

GREMIO.

A husband! a devil.

HORTENSIO.

I say, a husband.

GREMIO.

I say, a devil. Thinkest thou, Hortensio, though her father be very rich, any man is so very a fool to be married to hell?

HORTENSIO.

Tush, Gremio! Though it pass your patience and mine to endure her loud alarums, why, man, there be good fellows in the world, and a man could light on them, would take her with all faults, and money enough.

GREMIO.

I cannot tell; but I had as lief take her dowry with this condition: to be whipp'd at the high cross every morning.

HORTENSIO.

Faith, as you say, there's small choice in rotten apples. But come; since this bar in law makes us friends, it shall be so far forth friendly maintained, till by helping Baptista's eldest daughter to a husband, we set his youngest free for a husband, and then have to't afresh. Sweet Bianca! Happy man be his dole! He that runs fastest gets the ring. How say you, Signior Gremio?

GREMIO.

I am agreed; and would I had given him the best horse in Padua to begin his wooing, that would thoroughly woo her, wed her, and bed her, and rid the house of her. Come on.

[Exeunt Gremio and Hortensio.]

TRANIO.

I pray, sir, tell me, is it possible

That love should of a sudden take such hold?

LUCENTIO.

O Tranio! till I found it to be true,

I never thought it possible or likely;

But see, while idly I stood looking on,

I found the effect of love in idleness;

And now in plainness do confess to thee,

That art to me as secret and as dear

As Anna to the Queen of Carthage was,

Tranio, I burn, I pine, I perish, Tranio,

If I achieve not this young modest girl.

Counsel me, Tranio, for I know thou canst:

Assist me, Tranio, for I know thou wilt.

TRANIO.

Master, it is no time to chide you now;

Affection is not rated from the heart:

If love have touch'd you, nought remains but so:

Redime te captum quam queas minimo.

LUCENTIO.

Gramercies, lad; go forward; this contents;

The rest will comfort, for thy counsel's sound.

TRANIO.

Master, you look'd so longly on the maid.

Perhaps you mark'd not what's the pith of all.

LUCENTIO.

O, yes, I saw sweet beauty in her face,

Such as the daughter of Agenor had,

That made great Jove to humble him to her hand,

When with his knees he kiss'd the Cretan strand.

TRANIO.

Saw you no more? mark'd you not how her sister

Began to scold and raise up such a storm

That mortal ears might hardly endure the din?

LUCENTIO.

Tranio, I saw her coral lips to move,

And with her breath she did perfume the air;

37

Sacred and sweet was all I saw in her.

TRANIO.

Nay, then, 'tis time to stir him from his trance.

I pray, awake, sir: if you love the maid,

Bend thoughts and wits to achieve her. Thus it stands:

Her elder sister is so curst and shrewd,

That till the father rid his hands of her,

Master, your love must live a maid at home;

And therefore has he closely mew'd her up,

Because she will not be annoy'd with suitors.

LUCENTIO.

Ah, Tranio, what a cruel father's he!

But art thou not advis'd he took some care

To get her cunning schoolmasters to instruct her?

TRANIO.

Ay, marry, am I, sir, and now 'tis plotted.

LUCENTIO.

I have it, Tranio.

TRANIO.

Master, for my hand,

Both our inventions meet and jump in one.

LUCENTIO.

Tell me thine first.

TRANIO.

You will be schoolmaster,

And undertake the teaching of the maid:

That's your device.

LUCENTIO.

It is: may it be done?

TRANIO.

Not possible; for who shall bear your part

And be in Padua here Vincentio's son;

Keep house and ply his book, welcome his friends;

Visit his countrymen, and banquet them?

LUCENTIO.

Basta, content thee, for I have it full.

We have not yet been seen in any house,

Nor can we be distinguish'd by our faces

For man or master: then it follows thus:

Thou shalt be master, Tranio, in my stead,

Keep house and port and servants, as I should;

I will some other be; some Florentine,

Some Neapolitan, or meaner man of Pisa.

'Tis hatch'd, and shall be so: Tranio, at once

Uncase thee; take my colour'd hat and cloak.

When Biondello comes, he waits on thee;

But I will charm him first to keep his tongue.

[They exchange habits]

TRANIO.

So had you need.

In brief, sir, sith it your pleasure is,

And I am tied to be obedient;

For so your father charg'd me at our parting,

'Be serviceable to my son,' quoth he,

Although I think 'twas in another sense:

I am content to be Lucentio,

Because so well I love Lucentio.

LUCENTIO.

Tranio, be so, because Lucentio loves;

And let me be a slave, to achieve that maid

Whose sudden sight hath thrall'd my wounded eye.

Enter Biondello.

Here comes the rogue. Sirrah, where have you been?

BIONDELLO.

Where have I been? Nay, how now! where are you?

Master, has my fellow Tranio stol'n your clothes?

Or you stol'n his? or both? Pray, what's the news?

LUCENTIO.

Sirrah, come hither: 'tis no time to jest,

And therefore frame your manners to the time.

Your fellow Tranio here, to save my life,

Puts my apparel and my count'nance on,

And I for my escape have put on his;

For in a quarrel since I came ashore

I kill'd a man, and fear I was descried.

Wait you on him, I charge you, as becomes,

While I make way from hence to save my life.

You understand me?

BIONDELLO.

I, sir! Ne'er a whit.

LUCENTIO.

And not a jot of Tranio in your mouth:

Tranio is changed to Lucentio.

BIONDELLO.

The better for him: would I were so too!

TRANIO.

So could I, faith, boy, to have the next wish after,

That Lucentio indeed had Baptista's youngest daughter.

But, sirrah, not for my sake but your master's, I advise

You use your manners discreetly in all kind of companies:

When I am alone, why, then I am Tranio;

But in all places else your master, Lucentio.

LUCENTIO.

Tranio, let's go.

One thing more rests, that thyself execute,

To make one among these wooers: if thou ask me why,

Sufficeth my reasons are both good and weighty.

[Exeunt.]

[The Presenters above speak.]

FIRST SERVANT.

My lord, you nod; you do not mind the play.

SLY.

Yes, by Saint Anne, I do. A good matter, surely: comes there any more of it?

PAGE.

My lord, 'tis but begun.

SLY.

'Tis a very excellent piece of work, madam lady: would 'twere done!

[They sit and mark.]

SCENE II. Padua. Before HORTENSIO'S house.

Enter Petruchio and his man Grumio.

PETRUCHIO.

Verona, for a while I take my leave,

To see my friends in Padua; but of all

My best beloved and approved friend,

Hortensio; and I trow this is his house.

Here, sirrah Grumio, knock, I say.

GRUMIO.

Knock, sir? Whom should I knock? Is there any man has rebused your worship?

PETRUCHIO.

Villain, I say, knock me here soundly.

GRUMIO.

Knock you here, sir? Why, sir, what am I, sir, that I should knock you here, sir?

PETRUCHIO.

Villain, I say, knock me at this gate;

And rap me well, or I'll knock your knave's pate.

GRUMIO.

My master is grown quarrelsome. I should knock you first,

And then I know after who comes by the worst.

PETRUCHIO.

Will it not be?

Faith, sirrah, and you'll not knock, I'll ring it;

I'll try how you can sol, fa, and sing it.

[He wrings Grumio by the ears.]

GRUMIO.

Help, masters, help! my master is mad.

PETRUCHIO.

Now, knock when I bid you, sirrah villain!

Enter Hortensio.

HORTENSIO.

How now! what's the matter? My old friend Grumio! and my good friend Petruchio! How do you all at Verona?

PETRUCHIO.

Signior Hortensio, come you to part the fray?

Con tutto il cuore ben trovato, may I say.

HORTENSIO.

Alla nostra casa ben venuto; molto honorato signor mio Petruchio.

Rise, Grumio, rise: we will compound this quarrel.

GRUMIO.

Nay, 'tis no matter, sir, what he 'leges in Latin. If this be not a lawful cause for me to leave his service, look you, sir, he bid me knock him and rap him soundly, sir: well, was it fit for a servant to use his master so; being, perhaps, for aught I see, two-and-thirty, a pip out? Whom would to God I had well knock'd at first, then had not Grumio come by the worst.

PETRUCHIO.

A senseless villain! Good Hortensio,

I bade the rascal knock upon your gate,

And could not get him for my heart to do it.

GRUMIO.

Knock at the gate! O heavens! Spake you not these words plain: 'Sirrah knock me here, rap me here, knock me well, and knock me soundly'? And come you now with 'knocking at the gate'?

PETRUCHIO.

Sirrah, be gone, or talk not, I advise you.

HORTENSIO.

Petruchio, patience; I am Grumio's pledge;

Why, this's a heavy chance 'twixt him and you,

Your ancient, trusty, pleasant servant Grumio.

And tell me now, sweet friend, what happy gale

Blows you to Padua here from old Verona?

PETRUCHIO.

Such wind as scatters young men through the world

To seek their fortunes farther than at home,

Where small experience grows. But in a few,

Signior Hortensio, thus it stands with me:

Antonio, my father, is deceas'd,

And I have thrust myself into this maze,

Haply to wive and thrive as best I may;

Crowns in my purse I have, and goods at home,

And so am come abroad to see the world.

HORTENSIO.

Petruchio, shall I then come roundly to thee

And wish thee to a shrewd ill-favour'd wife?

Thou'dst thank me but a little for my counsel;

And yet I'll promise thee she shall be rich,

And very rich: but th'art too much my friend,

And I'll not wish thee to her.

PETRUCHIO.

Signior Hortensio, 'twixt such friends as we

Few words suffice; and therefore, if thou know

One rich enough to be Petruchio's wife,

As wealth is burden of my wooing dance,

Be she as foul as was Florentius' love,

As old as Sibyl, and as curst and shrewd

As Socrates' Xanthippe or a worse,

She moves me not, or not removes, at least,

Affection's edge in me, were she as rough

As are the swelling Adriatic seas:

I come to wive it wealthily in Padua;

If wealthily, then happily in Padua.

GRUMIO.

Nay, look you, sir, he tells you flatly what his mind is: why, give him gold enough and marry him to a puppet or an aglet-baby; or an old trot with ne'er a tooth in her head, though she have as many diseases as two-and-fifty horses: why, nothing comes amiss, so money comes withal.

HORTENSIO.

Petruchio, since we are stepp'd thus far in,

I will continue that I broach'd in jest.

I can, Petruchio, help thee to a wife

With wealth enough, and young and beauteous;

Brought up as best becomes a gentlewoman:

Her only fault,—and that is faults enough,—

Is, that she is intolerable curst,

And shrewd and froward, so beyond all measure,

That, were my state far worser than it is,

I would not wed her for a mine of gold.

PETRUCHIO.

Hortensio, peace! thou know'st not gold's effect:

Tell me her father's name, and 'tis enough;

For I will board her, though she chide as loud

As thunder when the clouds in autumn crack.

HORTENSIO.

Her father is Baptista Minola,

An affable and courteous gentleman;

Her name is Katherina Minola,

Renown'd in Padua for her scolding tongue.

PETRUCHIO.

I know her father, though I know not her;

And he knew my deceased father well.

I will not sleep, Hortensio, till I see her;

And therefore let me be thus bold with you,

To give you over at this first encounter,

Unless you will accompany me thither.

GRUMIO.

I pray you, sir, let him go while the humour lasts. O' my word, and she knew him as well as I do, she would think scolding would do little good upon him. She may perhaps call him half a score knaves or so; why, that's nothing; and he begin once, he'll rail in his rope-tricks. I'll tell you what, sir, and she stand him but a little, he will throw a figure in her face, and so disfigure her with it that she shall have no more eyes to see withal than a cat. You know him not, sir.

HORTENSIO.

Tarry, Petruchio, I must go with thee,

For in Baptista's keep my treasure is:

He hath the jewel of my life in hold,

His youngest daughter, beautiful Bianca,

And her withholds from me and other more,

Suitors to her and rivals in my love;

Supposing it a thing impossible,

For those defects I have before rehears'd,

That ever Katherina will be woo'd:

Therefore this order hath Baptista ta'en,

That none shall have access unto Bianca

Till Katherine the curst have got a husband.

GRUMIO.

Katherine the curst!

A title for a maid of all titles the worst.

HORTENSIO.

Now shall my friend Petruchio do me grace,

And offer me disguis'd in sober robes,

To old Baptista as a schoolmaster

Well seen in music, to instruct Bianca;

That so I may, by this device at least

Have leave and leisure to make love to her,

And unsuspected court her by herself.

GRUMIO.

Here's no knavery! See, to beguile the old folks, how the young folks lay their heads together!

Enter Gremio and Lucentio disguised, with books under his arm.

Master, master, look about you: who goes there, ha?

HORTENSIO.

Peace, Grumio! It is the rival of my love. Petruchio, stand by awhile.

GRUMIO.

A proper stripling, and an amorous!

GREMIO.

O! very well; I have perus'd the note.

Hark you, sir; I'll have them very fairly bound:

All books of love, see that at any hand,

And see you read no other lectures to her.

You understand me. Over and beside

Signior Baptista's liberality,

I'll mend it with a largess. Take your papers too,

And let me have them very well perfum'd;

For she is sweeter than perfume itself

To whom they go to. What will you read to her?

LUCENTIO.

Whate'er I read to her, I'll plead for you,

As for my patron, stand you so assur'd,

As firmly as yourself were still in place;

Yea, and perhaps with more successful words

Than you, unless you were a scholar, sir.

GREMIO.

O! this learning, what a thing it is.

GRUMIO.

O! this woodcock, what an ass it is.

PETRUCHIO.

Peace, sirrah!

HORTENSIO.

Grumio, mum! God save you, Signior Gremio!

GREMIO.

And you are well met, Signior Hortensio.

Trow you whither I am going? To Baptista Minola.

I promis'd to enquire carefully

About a schoolmaster for the fair Bianca;

And by good fortune I have lighted well

On this young man; for learning and behaviour

Fit for her turn, well read in poetry

And other books, good ones, I warrant ye.

HORTENSIO.

'Tis well; and I have met a gentleman

Hath promis'd me to help me to another,

A fine musician to instruct our mistress:

So shall I no whit be behind in duty

To fair Bianca, so belov'd of me.

GREMIO.

Belov'd of me, and that my deeds shall prove.

GRUMIO.

[Aside.] And that his bags shall prove.

HORTENSIO.

Gremio, 'tis now no time to vent our love:

Listen to me, and if you speak me fair,

I'll tell you news indifferent good for either.

Here is a gentleman whom by chance I met,

Upon agreement from us to his liking,

Will undertake to woo curst Katherine;

Yea, and to marry her, if her dowry please.

GREMIO.

So said, so done, is well.

Hortensio, have you told him all her faults?

PETRUCHIO.

I know she is an irksome brawling scold;

If that be all, masters, I hear no harm.

GREMIO.

No, say'st me so, friend? What countryman?

PETRUCHIO.

Born in Verona, old Antonio's son.

My father dead, my fortune lives for me;

And I do hope good days and long to see.

GREMIO.

O sir, such a life, with such a wife, were strange!

But if you have a stomach, to't a God's name;

You shall have me assisting you in all.

But will you woo this wild-cat?

PETRUCHIO.

Will I live?

GRUMIO.

Will he woo her? Ay, or I'll hang her.

PETRUCHIO.

Why came I hither but to that intent?

Think you a little din can daunt mine ears?

Have I not in my time heard lions roar?

Have I not heard the sea, puff'd up with winds,

Rage like an angry boar chafed with sweat?

Have I not heard great ordnance in the field,

And heaven's artillery thunder in the skies?

Have I not in a pitched battle heard

Loud 'larums, neighing steeds, and trumpets' clang?

And do you tell me of a woman's tongue,

That gives not half so great a blow to hear

As will a chestnut in a farmer's fire?

Tush, tush! fear boys with bugs.

GRUMIO.

[Aside] For he fears none.

GREMIO.

Hortensio, hark:

This gentleman is happily arriv'd,

My mind presumes, for his own good and yours.

HORTENSIO.

I promis'd we would be contributors,

And bear his charge of wooing, whatsoe'er.

GREMIO.

And so we will, provided that he win her.

GRUMIO.

I would I were as sure of a good dinner.

Enter Tranio brave, and Biondello.

TRANIO.

Gentlemen, God save you! If I may be bold,

Tell me, I beseech you, which is the readiest way

To the house of Signior Baptista Minola?

BIONDELLO.

He that has the two fair daughters; is't he you mean?

TRANIO.

Even he, Biondello!

GREMIO.

Hark you, sir, you mean not her to—

TRANIO.

Perhaps him and her, sir; what have you to do?

PETRUCHIO.

Not her that chides, sir, at any hand, I pray.

TRANIO.

I love no chiders, sir. Biondello, let's away.

LUCENTIO.

[Aside] Well begun, Tranio.

HORTENSIO.

Sir, a word ere you go.

Are you a suitor to the maid you talk of, yea or no?

TRANIO.

And if I be, sir, is it any offence?

GREMIO.

No; if without more words you will get you hence.

TRANIO.

Why, sir, I pray, are not the streets as free

For me as for you?

GREMIO.

But so is not she.

TRANIO.

For what reason, I beseech you?

GREMIO.

For this reason, if you'll know,

That she's the choice love of Signior Gremio.

HORTENSIO.

That she's the chosen of Signior Hortensio.

TRANIO.

Softly, my masters! If you be gentlemen,

Do me this right; hear me with patience.

Baptista is a noble gentleman,

To whom my father is not all unknown;

And were his daughter fairer than she is,

She may more suitors have, and me for one.

Fair Leda's daughter had a thousand wooers;

Then well one more may fair Bianca have;

And so she shall: Lucentio shall make one,

Though Paris came in hope to speed alone.

GREMIO.

What, this gentleman will out-talk us all.

LUCENTIO.

Sir, give him head; I know he'll prove a jade.

PETRUCHIO.

Hortensio, to what end are all these words?

HORTENSIO.

Sir, let me be so bold as ask you,

Did you yet ever see Baptista's daughter?

TRANIO.

No, sir, but hear I do that he hath two,

The one as famous for a scolding tongue

As is the other for beauteous modesty.

PETRUCHIO.

Sir, sir, the first's for me; let her go by.

GREMIO.

Yea, leave that labour to great Hercules,

And let it be more than Alcides' twelve.

PETRUCHIO.

Sir, understand you this of me, in sooth:

The youngest daughter, whom you hearken for,

Her father keeps from all access of suitors,

And will not promise her to any man

Until the elder sister first be wed;

The younger then is free, and not before.

TRANIO.

If it be so, sir, that you are the man

Must stead us all, and me amongst the rest;

And if you break the ice, and do this feat,

Achieve the elder, set the younger free

For our access, whose hap shall be to have her

Will not so graceless be to be ingrate.

HORTENSIO.

Sir, you say well, and well you do conceive;

And since you do profess to be a suitor,

You must, as we do, gratify this gentleman,

To whom we all rest generally beholding.

TRANIO.

Sir, I shall not be slack; in sign whereof,

Please ye we may contrive this afternoon,

And quaff carouses to our mistress' health;

And do as adversaries do in law,

Strive mightily, but eat and drink as friends.

GRUMIO, BIONDELLO.

O excellent motion! Fellows, let's be gone.

HORTENSIO.

The motion's good indeed, and be it so:—

Petruchio, I shall be your ben venuto.

[Exeunt.]

ACT II

SCENE I. Padua. A room in BAPTISTA'S house.

Enter Katherina and Bianca.

BIANCA.

Good sister, wrong me not, nor wrong yourself,

To make a bondmaid and a slave of me;

That I disdain; but for these other gawds,

Unbind my hands, I'll pull them off myself,

Yea, all my raiment, to my petticoat;

Or what you will command me will I do,

So well I know my duty to my elders.

KATHERINA.

Of all thy suitors here I charge thee tell

Whom thou lov'st best: see thou dissemble not.

BIANCA.

Believe me, sister, of all the men alive

I never yet beheld that special face

Which I could fancy more than any other.

KATHERINA.

Minion, thou liest. Is't not Hortensio?

BIANCA.

If you affect him, sister, here I swear

I'll plead for you myself but you shall have him.

KATHERINA.

O! then, belike, you fancy riches more:

You will have Gremio to keep you fair.

BIANCA.

Is it for him you do envy me so?

Nay, then you jest; and now I well perceive

You have but jested with me all this while:

I prithee, sister Kate, untie my hands.

KATHERINA.

If that be jest, then all the rest was so.

[Strikes her.]

Enter Baptista.

BAPTISTA.

Why, how now, dame! Whence grows this insolence?

Bianca, stand aside. Poor girl! she weeps.

Go ply thy needle; meddle not with her.

For shame, thou hilding of a devilish spirit,

Why dost thou wrong her that did ne'er wrong thee?

When did she cross thee with a bitter word?

KATHERINA.

Her silence flouts me, and I'll be reveng'd.

[Flies after Bianca.]

BAPTISTA.

What! in my sight? Bianca, get thee in.

[Exit Bianca.]

KATHERINA.

What! will you not suffer me? Nay, now I see

She is your treasure, she must have a husband;

I must dance bare-foot on her wedding-day,

And, for your love to her, lead apes in hell.

Talk not to me: I will go sit and weep

Till I can find occasion of revenge.

[Exit.]

BAPTISTA.

Was ever gentleman thus griev'd as I?

But who comes here?

Enter Gremio, with Lucentio in the habit of a mean man; Petruchio, with Hortensio as a musician; and Tranio, with Biondello bearing a lute and books.

GREMIO.

Good morrow, neighbour Baptista.

BAPTISTA.

Good morrow, neighbour Gremio. God save you, gentlemen!

PETRUCHIO.

And you, good sir! Pray, have you not a daughter

Call'd Katherina, fair and virtuous?

BAPTISTA.

I have a daughter, sir, call'd Katherina.

GREMIO.

You are too blunt: go to it orderly.

PETRUCHIO.

You wrong me, Signior Gremio: give me leave.

I am a gentleman of Verona, sir,

That, hearing of her beauty and her wit,

Her affability and bashful modesty,

Her wondrous qualities and mild behaviour,

Am bold to show myself a forward guest

Within your house, to make mine eye the witness

Of that report which I so oft have heard.

And, for an entrance to my entertainment,

I do present you with a man of mine,

[Presenting Hortensio.]

Cunning in music and the mathematics,

To instruct her fully in those sciences,

Whereof I know she is not ignorant.

Accept of him, or else you do me wrong:

His name is Licio, born in Mantua.

BAPTISTA.

Y'are welcome, sir, and he for your good sake;

But for my daughter Katherine, this I know,

She is not for your turn, the more my grief.

PETRUCHIO.

I see you do not mean to part with her;

Or else you like not of my company.

BAPTISTA.

Mistake me not; I speak but as I find.

Whence are you, sir? What may I call your name?

PETRUCHIO.

Petruchio is my name, Antonio's son;

A man well known throughout all Italy.

BAPTISTA.

I know him well: you are welcome for his sake.

GREMIO.

Saving your tale, Petruchio, I pray,

Let us, that are poor petitioners, speak too.

Backare! you are marvellous forward.

PETRUCHIO.

O, pardon me, Signior Gremio; I would fain be doing.

GREMIO.

I doubt it not, sir; but you will curse your wooing. Neighbour, this is a gift very grateful, I am sure of it. To express the like kindness, myself, that have been more kindly beholding to you than any, freely give unto you this young scholar,

[Presenting Lucentio.]

that has been long studying at Rheims; as cunning in Greek, Latin, and other languages, as the other in music and mathematics. His name is Cambio; pray accept his service.

BAPTISTA.

A thousand thanks, Signior Gremio; welcome, good Cambio. [To Tranio.] But, gentle sir, methinks you walk like a stranger. May I be so bold to know the cause of your coming?

TRANIO.

Pardon me, sir, the boldness is mine own,

That, being a stranger in this city here,

Do make myself a suitor to your daughter,

Unto Bianca, fair and virtuous.

Nor is your firm resolve unknown to me,

In the preferment of the eldest sister.

This liberty is all that I request,

That, upon knowledge of my parentage,

I may have welcome 'mongst the rest that woo,

And free access and favour as the rest:

And, toward the education of your daughters,

I here bestow a simple instrument,

And this small packet of Greek and Latin books:

If you accept them, then their worth is great.

BAPTISTA.

Lucentio is your name, of whence, I pray?

TRANIO.

Of Pisa, sir; son to Vincentio.

BAPTISTA.

A mighty man of Pisa: by report

I know him well: you are very welcome, sir.

[To Hortensio.] Take you the lute,

[To Lucentio.] and you the set of books;

You shall go see your pupils presently.

Holla, within!

Enter a Servant.

Sirrah, lead these gentlemen

To my daughters, and tell them both

These are their tutors: bid them use them well.

[Exeunt Servant with Hortensio, Lucentio and Biondello.]

We will go walk a little in the orchard,

And then to dinner. You are passing welcome,

And so I pray you all to think yourselves.

PETRUCHIO.

Signior Baptista, my business asketh haste,

And every day I cannot come to woo.

You knew my father well, and in him me,

Left solely heir to all his lands and goods,

Which I have bettered rather than decreas'd:

Then tell me, if I get your daughter's love,

What dowry shall I have with her to wife?

BAPTISTA.

After my death, the one half of my lands,

And in possession twenty thousand crowns.

PETRUCHIO.

And, for that dowry, I'll assure her of

Her widowhood, be it that she survive me,

In all my lands and leases whatsoever.

Let specialities be therefore drawn between us,

That covenants may be kept on either hand.

BAPTISTA.

Ay, when the special thing is well obtain'd,

That is, her love; for that is all in all.

PETRUCHIO.

Why, that is nothing; for I tell you, father,

I am as peremptory as she proud-minded;

And where two raging fires meet together,

They do consume the thing that feeds their fury:

Though little fire grows great with little wind,

Yet extreme gusts will blow out fire and all;

So I to her, and so she yields to me;

For I am rough and woo not like a babe.

BAPTISTA.

Well mayst thou woo, and happy be thy speed!

But be thou arm'd for some unhappy words.

PETRUCHIO.

Ay, to the proof, as mountains are for winds,

That shake not though they blow perpetually.

Re-enter Hortensio, with his head broke.

BAPTISTA.

How now, my friend! Why dost thou look so pale?

HORTENSIO.

For fear, I promise you, if I look pale.

BAPTISTA.

What, will my daughter prove a good musician?

HORTENSIO.

I think she'll sooner prove a soldier:

Iron may hold with her, but never lutes.

BAPTISTA.

Why, then thou canst not break her to the lute?

HORTENSIO.

Why, no; for she hath broke the lute to me.

I did but tell her she mistook her frets,

And bow'd her hand to teach her fingering;

When, with a most impatient devilish spirit,

'Frets, call you these?' quoth she 'I'll fume with them';

And with that word she struck me on the head,

And through the instrument my pate made way;

And there I stood amazed for a while,

As on a pillory, looking through the lute;

While she did call me rascal fiddler,

And twangling Jack, with twenty such vile terms,

As had she studied to misuse me so.

PETRUCHIO.

Now, by the world, it is a lusty wench!

I love her ten times more than e'er I did:

O! how I long to have some chat with her!

BAPTISTA.

[To Hortensio.] Well, go with me, and be not so discomfited;

Proceed in practice with my younger daughter;

She's apt to learn, and thankful for good turns.

Signior Petruchio, will you go with us,

Or shall I send my daughter Kate to you?

PETRUCHIO.

I pray you do.

      [Exeunt Baptista, Gremio, Tranio and Hortensio.]

I will attend her here,

And woo her with some spirit when she comes.

Say that she rail; why, then I'll tell her plain

She sings as sweetly as a nightingale:

Say that she frown; I'll say she looks as clear

As morning roses newly wash'd with dew:

Say she be mute, and will not speak a word;

Then I'll commend her volubility,

And say she uttereth piercing eloquence:

If she do bid me pack, I'll give her thanks,

As though she bid me stay by her a week:

If she deny to wed, I'll crave the day

When I shall ask the banns, and when be married.

But here she comes; and now, Petruchio, speak.

Enter Katherina.

Good morrow, Kate; for that's your name, I hear.

KATHERINA.

Well have you heard, but something hard of hearing:

They call me Katherine that do talk of me.

PETRUCHIO.

You lie, in faith, for you are call'd plain Kate,

And bonny Kate, and sometimes Kate the curst;

But, Kate, the prettiest Kate in Christendom,

Kate of Kate Hall, my super-dainty Kate,

For dainties are all Kates, and therefore, Kate,

Take this of me, Kate of my consolation;

Hearing thy mildness prais'd in every town,

Thy virtues spoke of, and thy beauty sounded,—

Yet not so deeply as to thee belongs,—

Myself am mov'd to woo thee for my wife.

KATHERINA.

Mov'd! in good time: let him that mov'd you hither

Remove you hence. I knew you at the first,

You were a moveable.

PETRUCHIO.

Why, what's a moveable?

KATHERINA.

A joint-stool.

PETRUCHIO.

Thou hast hit it: come, sit on me.

KATHERINA.

Asses are made to bear, and so are you.

PETRUCHIO.

Women are made to bear, and so are you.

KATHERINA.

No such jade as bear you, if me you mean.

PETRUCHIO.

Alas! good Kate, I will not burden thee;

For, knowing thee to be but young and light,—

KATHERINA.

Too light for such a swain as you to catch;

And yet as heavy as my weight should be.

PETRUCHIO.

Should be! should buz!

KATHERINA.

Well ta'en, and like a buzzard.

PETRUCHIO.

O, slow-wing'd turtle! shall a buzzard take thee?

KATHERINA.

Ay, for a turtle, as he takes a buzzard.

PETRUCHIO.

Come, come, you wasp; i' faith, you are too angry.

KATHERINA.

If I be waspish, best beware my sting.

PETRUCHIO.

My remedy is then to pluck it out.

KATHERINA.

Ay, if the fool could find it where it lies.

PETRUCHIO.

Who knows not where a wasp does wear his sting?

In his tail.

KATHERINA.

In his tongue.

PETRUCHIO.

Whose tongue?

KATHERINA.

Yours, if you talk of tales; and so farewell.

PETRUCHIO.

What! with my tongue in your tail? Nay, come again,

Good Kate; I am a gentleman.

KATHERINA.

That I'll try.

[Striking him.]

PETRUCHIO.

I swear I'll cuff you if you strike again.

KATHERINA.

So may you lose your arms:

If you strike me, you are no gentleman;

And if no gentleman, why then no arms.

PETRUCHIO.

A herald, Kate? O! put me in thy books.

KATHERINA.

What is your crest? a coxcomb?

PETRUCHIO.

A combless cock, so Kate will be my hen.

KATHERINA.

No cock of mine; you crow too like a craven.

PETRUCHIO.

Nay, come, Kate, come; you must not look so sour.

KATHERINA.

It is my fashion when I see a crab.

PETRUCHIO.

Why, here's no crab, and therefore look not sour.

KATHERINA.

There is, there is.

PETRUCHIO.

Then show it me.

KATHERINA.

Had I a glass I would.

PETRUCHIO.

What, you mean my face?

KATHERINA.

Well aim'd of such a young one.

PETRUCHIO.

Now, by Saint George, I am too young for you.

KATHERINA.

Yet you are wither'd.

PETRUCHIO.

'Tis with cares.

KATHERINA.

I care not.

PETRUCHIO.

Nay, hear you, Kate: in sooth, you 'scape not so.

KATHERINA.

I chafe you, if I tarry; let me go.

PETRUCHIO.

No, not a whit; I find you passing gentle.

'Twas told me you were rough, and coy, and sullen,

And now I find report a very liar;

For thou art pleasant, gamesome, passing courteous,

But slow in speech, yet sweet as spring-time flowers.

Thou canst not frown, thou canst not look askance,

Nor bite the lip, as angry wenches will,

Nor hast thou pleasure to be cross in talk;

But thou with mildness entertain'st thy wooers;

With gentle conference, soft and affable.

Why does the world report that Kate doth limp?

O sland'rous world! Kate like the hazel-twig

Is straight and slender, and as brown in hue

As hazel-nuts, and sweeter than the kernels.

O! let me see thee walk: thou dost not halt.

KATHERINA.

Go, fool, and whom thou keep'st command.

PETRUCHIO.

Did ever Dian so become a grove

As Kate this chamber with her princely gait?

O! be thou Dian, and let her be Kate,

And then let Kate be chaste, and Dian sportful!

KATHERINA.

Where did you study all this goodly speech?

PETRUCHIO.

It is extempore, from my mother-wit.

KATHERINA.

A witty mother! witless else her son.

PETRUCHIO.

Am I not wise?

KATHERINA.

Yes; keep you warm.

PETRUCHIO.

Marry, so I mean, sweet Katherine, in thy bed;

And therefore, setting all this chat aside,

Thus in plain terms: your father hath consented

That you shall be my wife your dowry 'greed on;

And will you, nill you, I will marry you.

Now, Kate, I am a husband for your turn;

For, by this light, whereby I see thy beauty,—

Thy beauty that doth make me like thee well,—

Thou must be married to no man but me;

For I am he am born to tame you, Kate,

And bring you from a wild Kate to a Kate

Conformable as other household Kates.

Re-enter Baptista, Gremio and Tranio.

Here comes your father. Never make denial;

I must and will have Katherine to my wife.

BAPTISTA.

Now, Signior Petruchio, how speed you with my daughter?

PETRUCHIO.

How but well, sir? how but well?

It were impossible I should speed amiss.

BAPTISTA.

Why, how now, daughter Katherine, in your dumps?

KATHERINA.

Call you me daughter? Now I promise you

You have show'd a tender fatherly regard

To wish me wed to one half lunatic,

A mad-cap ruffian and a swearing Jack,

That thinks with oaths to face the matter out.

PETRUCHIO.

Father, 'tis thus: yourself and all the world

That talk'd of her have talk'd amiss of her:

If she be curst, it is for policy,

For she's not froward, but modest as the dove;

She is not hot, but temperate as the morn;

For patience she will prove a second Grissel,

And Roman Lucrece for her chastity;

And to conclude, we have 'greed so well together

That upon Sunday is the wedding-day.

KATHERINA.

I'll see thee hang'd on Sunday first.

GREMIO.

Hark, Petruchio; she says she'll see thee hang'd first.

TRANIO.

Is this your speeding? Nay, then good-night our part!

PETRUCHIO.

Be patient, gentlemen. I choose her for myself;

If she and I be pleas'd, what's that to you?

'Tis bargain'd 'twixt us twain, being alone,

That she shall still be curst in company.

I tell you, 'tis incredible to believe

How much she loves me: O! the kindest Kate

She hung about my neck, and kiss on kiss

She vied so fast, protesting oath on oath,

That in a twink she won me to her love.

O! you are novices: 'tis a world to see,

How tame, when men and women are alone,

A meacock wretch can make the curstest shrew.

Give me thy hand, Kate; I will unto Venice,

To buy apparel 'gainst the wedding-day.

Provide the feast, father, and bid the guests;

I will be sure my Katherine shall be fine.

BAPTISTA.

I know not what to say; but give me your hands.

God send you joy, Petruchio! 'Tis a match.

GREMIO, TRANIO.

Amen, say we; we will be witnesses.

PETRUCHIO.

Father, and wife, and gentlemen, adieu.

I will to Venice; Sunday comes apace;

We will have rings and things, and fine array;

And kiss me, Kate; we will be married o' Sunday.

[Exeunt Petruchio and Katherina, severally.]

GREMIO.

Was ever match clapp'd up so suddenly?

BAPTISTA.

Faith, gentlemen, now I play a merchant's part,

And venture madly on a desperate mart.

TRANIO.

'Twas a commodity lay fretting by you;

'Twill bring you gain, or perish on the seas.

BAPTISTA.

The gain I seek is, quiet in the match.

GREMIO.

No doubt but he hath got a quiet catch.

But now, Baptista, to your younger daughter:

Now is the day we long have looked for;

I am your neighbour, and was suitor first.

TRANIO.

And I am one that love Bianca more

Than words can witness or your thoughts can guess.

GREMIO.

Youngling, thou canst not love so dear as I.

TRANIO.

Greybeard, thy love doth freeze.

GREMIO.

But thine doth fry.

Skipper, stand back; 'tis age that nourisheth.

TRANIO.

But youth in ladies' eyes that flourisheth.

BAPTISTA.

Content you, gentlemen; I'll compound this strife:

'Tis deeds must win the prize, and he of both

That can assure my daughter greatest dower

Shall have my Bianca's love.

Say, Signior Gremio, what can you assure her?

GREMIO.

First, as you know, my house within the city

Is richly furnished with plate and gold:

Basins and ewers to lave her dainty hands;

My hangings all of Tyrian tapestry;

In ivory coffers I have stuff'd my crowns;

In cypress chests my arras counterpoints,

Costly apparel, tents, and canopies,

Fine linen, Turkey cushions boss'd with pearl,

Valance of Venice gold in needlework;

Pewter and brass, and all things that belong

To house or housekeeping: then, at my farm

I have a hundred milch-kine to the pail,

Six score fat oxen standing in my stalls,

And all things answerable to this portion.

Myself am struck in years, I must confess;

And if I die tomorrow this is hers,

If whilst I live she will be only mine.

TRANIO.

That 'only' came well in. Sir, list to me:

I am my father's heir and only son;

If I may have your daughter to my wife,

I'll leave her houses three or four as good

Within rich Pisa's walls as anyone

Old Signior Gremio has in Padua;

Besides two thousand ducats by the year

Of fruitful land, all which shall be her jointure.

What, have I pinch'd you, Signior Gremio?

GREMIO.

Two thousand ducats by the year of land!

My land amounts not to so much in all:

That she shall have, besides an argosy

That now is lying in Marseilles' road.

What, have I chok'd you with an argosy?

TRANIO.

Gremio, 'tis known my father hath no less

Than three great argosies, besides two galliasses,

And twelve tight galleys; these I will assure her,

And twice as much, whate'er thou offer'st next.

GREMIO.

Nay, I have offer'd all; I have no more;

And she can have no more than all I have;

If you like me, she shall have me and mine.

TRANIO.

Why, then the maid is mine from all the world,

By your firm promise; Gremio is out-vied.

BAPTISTA.

I must confess your offer is the best;

And let your father make her the assurance,

She is your own; else, you must pardon me;

If you should die before him, where's her dower?

TRANIO.

That's but a cavil; he is old, I young.

GREMIO.

And may not young men die as well as old?

BAPTISTA.

Well, gentlemen,

I am thus resolv'd. On Sunday next, you know,

My daughter Katherine is to be married;

Now, on the Sunday following, shall Bianca

Be bride to you, if you make this assurance;

If not, to Signior Gremio.

And so I take my leave, and thank you both.

GREMIO.

Adieu, good neighbour.

[Exit Baptista.]

Now, I fear thee not:

Sirrah young gamester, your father were a fool

To give thee all, and in his waning age

Set foot under thy table. Tut! a toy!

An old Italian fox is not so kind, my boy.

[Exit.]

TRANIO.

A vengeance on your crafty wither'd hide!

Yet I have fac'd it with a card of ten.

'Tis in my head to do my master good:

I see no reason but suppos'd Lucentio

Must get a father, call'd suppos'd Vincentio;

And that's a wonder: fathers commonly

Do get their children; but in this case of wooing

A child shall get a sire, if I fail not of my cunning.

[Exit.]

ACT III

SCENE I. Padua. A room in BAPTISTA'S house.

Enter Lucentio, Hortensio and Bianca.

LUCENTIO.

Fiddler, forbear; you grow too forward, sir.

Have you so soon forgot the entertainment

Her sister Katherine welcome'd you withal?

HORTENSIO.

But, wrangling pedant, this is

The patroness of heavenly harmony:

Then give me leave to have prerogative;

And when in music we have spent an hour,

Your lecture shall have leisure for as much.

LUCENTIO.

Preposterous ass, that never read so far

To know the cause why music was ordain'd!

Was it not to refresh the mind of man

After his studies or his usual pain?

Then give me leave to read philosophy,

And while I pause serve in your harmony.

HORTENSIO.

Sirrah, I will not bear these braves of thine.

BIANCA.

Why, gentlemen, you do me double wrong,

To strive for that which resteth in my choice.

I am no breeching scholar in the schools,

I'll not be tied to hours nor 'pointed times,

But learn my lessons as I please myself.

And, to cut off all strife, here sit we down;

Take you your instrument, play you the whiles;

His lecture will be done ere you have tun'd.

HORTENSIO.

You'll leave his lecture when I am in tune?

[Retires.]

LUCENTIO.

That will be never: tune your instrument.

BIANCA.

Where left we last?

LUCENTIO.

Here, madam:—

Hic ibat Simois; hic est Sigeia tellus;

Hic steterat Priami regia celsa senis.

BIANCA.

Construe them.

LUCENTIO.

Hic ibat, as I told you before, Simois, I am Lucentio, hic est, son unto Vincentio of Pisa, Sigeia tellus, disguised thus to get your love, Hic steterat, and that Lucentio that comes a-wooing, Priami, is my man Tranio, regia, bearing my port, celsa senis, that we might beguile the old pantaloon.

HORTENSIO. [Returning.]

Madam, my instrument's in tune.

BIANCA.

Let's hear.—

[Hortensio plays.]

O fie! the treble jars.

LUCENTIO.

Spit in the hole, man, and tune again.

BIANCA.

Now let me see if I can construe it: Hic ibat Simois, I know you not; hic est Sigeia tellus, I trust you not; Hic steterat Priami, take heed he hear us not; regia, presume not; celsa senis, despair not.

HORTENSIO.

Madam, 'tis now in tune.

LUCENTIO.

All but the base.

HORTENSIO.

The base is right; 'tis the base knave that jars.

[Aside] How fiery and forward our pedant is!

Now, for my life, the knave doth court my love:

Pedascule, I'll watch you better yet.

BIANCA.

In time I may believe, yet I mistrust.

LUCENTIO.

Mistrust it not; for sure, Æacides

Was Ajax, call'd so from his grandfather.

BIANCA.

I must believe my master; else, I promise you,

I should be arguing still upon that doubt;

But let it rest. Now, Licio, to you.

Good master, take it not unkindly, pray,

That I have been thus pleasant with you both.

HORTENSIO.

[To Lucentio] You may go walk and give me leave a while;

My lessons make no music in three parts.

LUCENTIO.

Are you so formal, sir? Well, I must wait,

[Aside] And watch withal; for, but I be deceiv'd,

Our fine musician groweth amorous.

HORTENSIO.

Madam, before you touch the instrument,

To learn the order of my fingering,

I must begin with rudiments of art;

To teach you gamut in a briefer sort,

More pleasant, pithy, and effectual,

Than hath been taught by any of my trade:

And there it is in writing, fairly drawn.

BIANCA.

Why, I am past my gamut long ago.

HORTENSIO.

Yet read the gamut of Hortensio.

BIANCA.

Gamut I am, the ground of all accord,

A re, to plead Hortensio's passion;

B mi, Bianca, take him for thy lord,

C fa ut, that loves with all affection:

D sol re, one clef, two notes have I

E la mi, show pity or I die.

Call you this gamut? Tut, I like it not:

Old fashions please me best; I am not so nice,

To change true rules for odd inventions.

Enter a Servant.

SERVANT.

Mistress, your father prays you leave your books,

And help to dress your sister's chamber up:

You know tomorrow is the wedding-day.

BIANCA.

Farewell, sweet masters, both: I must be gone.

[Exeunt Bianca and Servant.]

LUCENTIO.

Faith, mistress, then I have no cause to stay.

[Exit.]

HORTENSIO.

But I have cause to pry into this pedant:

Methinks he looks as though he were in love.

Yet if thy thoughts, Bianca, be so humble

To cast thy wand'ring eyes on every stale,

Seize thee that list: if once I find thee ranging,

Hortensio will be quit with thee by changing.

[Exit.]

SCENE II. The same. Before BAPTISTA'S house.

Enter Baptista, Gremio, Tranio, Katherina, Bianca, Lucentio and Attendants.

BAPTISTA. [To Tranio.]

Signior Lucentio, this is the 'pointed day

That Katherine and Petruchio should be married,

And yet we hear not of our son-in-law.

What will be said? What mockery will it be

To want the bridegroom when the priest attends

To speak the ceremonial rites of marriage!

What says Lucentio to this shame of ours?

KATHERINA.

No shame but mine; I must, forsooth, be forc'd

To give my hand, oppos'd against my heart,

Unto a mad-brain rudesby, full of spleen;

Who woo'd in haste and means to wed at leisure.

I told you, I, he was a frantic fool,

Hiding his bitter jests in blunt behaviour;

And to be noted for a merry man,

He'll woo a thousand, 'point the day of marriage,

Make friends, invite, and proclaim the banns;

Yet never means to wed where he hath woo'd.

Now must the world point at poor Katherine,

And say 'Lo! there is mad Petruchio's wife,

If it would please him come and marry her.'

TRANIO.

Patience, good Katherine, and Baptista too.

Upon my life, Petruchio means but well,

Whatever fortune stays him from his word:

Though he be blunt, I know him passing wise;

Though he be merry, yet withal he's honest.

KATHERINA.

Would Katherine had never seen him though!

              [Exit weeping, followed by Bianca and others.]

BAPTISTA.

Go, girl, I cannot blame thee now to weep,

For such an injury would vex a very saint;

Much more a shrew of thy impatient humour.

Enter Biondello.

Master, master! News! old news, and such news as you never heard of!

BAPTISTA.

Is it new and old too? How may that be?

BIONDELLO.

Why, is it not news to hear of Petruchio's coming?

BAPTISTA.

Is he come?

BIONDELLO.

Why, no, sir.

BAPTISTA.

What then?

BIONDELLO.

He is coming.

BAPTISTA.

When will he be here?

BIONDELLO.

When he stands where I am and sees you there.

TRANIO.

But say, what to thine old news?

BIONDELLO.

Why, Petruchio is coming, in a new hat and an old jerkin; a pair of old breeches thrice turned; a pair of boots that have been candle-cases, one buckled, another laced; an old rusty sword ta'en out of the town armoury, with a broken hilt, and chapeless; with two broken points: his horse hipped with an old mothy saddle and stirrups of no kindred; besides, possessed with the glanders and like to mose in the chine; troubled with the lampass, infected with the fashions, full of windgalls, sped with spavins, rayed with the yellows, past cure of the fives, stark spoiled with the staggers, begnawn with the bots, swayed in the back and shoulder-shotten; near-legged before, and with a half-checked bit, and a head-stall of sheep's leather, which, being restrained to keep him from stumbling, hath been often burst, and now repaired with knots; one girth six times pieced, and a woman's crupper of velure, which hath two letters for her name fairly set down in studs, and here and there pieced with pack-thread.

BAPTISTA.

Who comes with him?

BIONDELLO.

O, sir! his lackey, for all the world caparisoned like the horse; with a linen stock on one leg and a kersey boot-hose on the other, gartered with a red and blue list; an old hat, and the humour of forty fancies prick'd in't for a feather: a monster, a very monster in apparel, and not like a Christian footboy or a gentleman's lackey.

TRANIO.

'Tis some odd humour pricks him to this fashion;

Yet oftentimes lie goes but mean-apparell'd.

BAPTISTA.

I am glad he's come, howsoe'er he comes.

BIONDELLO.

Why, sir, he comes not.

BAPTISTA.

Didst thou not say he comes?

BIONDELLO.

Who? that Petruchio came?

BAPTISTA.

Ay, that Petruchio came.

BIONDELLO.

No, sir; I say his horse comes, with him on his back.

BAPTISTA.

Why, that's all one.

BIONDELLO.

Nay, by Saint Jamy,

I hold you a penny,

A horse and a man

Is more than one,

And yet not many.

Enter Petruchio and Grumio.

PETRUCHIO.

Come, where be these gallants? Who is at home?

BAPTISTA.

You are welcome, sir.

PETRUCHIO.

And yet I come not well.

BAPTISTA.

And yet you halt not.

TRANIO.

Not so well apparell'd as I wish you were.

PETRUCHIO.

Were it better, I should rush in thus.

But where is Kate? Where is my lovely bride?

How does my father? Gentles, methinks you frown;

And wherefore gaze this goodly company,

As if they saw some wondrous monument,

Some comet or unusual prodigy?

BAPTISTA.

Why, sir, you know this is your wedding-day:

First were we sad, fearing you would not come;

Now sadder, that you come so unprovided.

Fie! doff this habit, shame to your estate,

An eye-sore to our solemn festival.

TRANIO.

And tell us what occasion of import

Hath all so long detain'd you from your wife,

And sent you hither so unlike yourself?

PETRUCHIO.

Tedious it were to tell, and harsh to hear;

Sufficeth I am come to keep my word,

Though in some part enforced to digress;

Which at more leisure I will so excuse

As you shall well be satisfied withal.

But where is Kate? I stay too long from her;

The morning wears, 'tis time we were at church.

TRANIO.

See not your bride in these unreverent robes;

Go to my chamber, put on clothes of mine.

PETRUCHIO.

Not I, believe me: thus I'll visit her.

BAPTISTA.

But thus, I trust, you will not marry her.

PETRUCHIO.

Good sooth, even thus; therefore ha' done with words;

To me she's married, not unto my clothes.

Could I repair what she will wear in me

As I can change these poor accoutrements,

'Twere well for Kate and better for myself.

But what a fool am I to chat with you

When I should bid good morrow to my bride,

And seal the title with a lovely kiss!

[Exeunt Petruchio, Grumio and Biondello.]

TRANIO.

He hath some meaning in his mad attire.

We will persuade him, be it possible,

To put on better ere he go to church.

BAPTISTA.

I'll after him and see the event of this.

[Exeunt Baptista, Gremio and Attendants.]

TRANIO.

But, sir, to love concerneth us to add

Her father's liking; which to bring to pass,

As I before imparted to your worship,

I am to get a man,—whate'er he be

It skills not much; we'll fit him to our turn,—

And he shall be Vincentio of Pisa,

And make assurance here in Padua,

Of greater sums than I have promised.

So shall you quietly enjoy your hope,

And marry sweet Bianca with consent.

LUCENTIO.

Were it not that my fellow schoolmaster

Doth watch Bianca's steps so narrowly,

'Twere good, methinks, to steal our marriage;

Which once perform'd, let all the world say no,

I'll keep mine own despite of all the world.

TRANIO.

That by degrees we mean to look into,

And watch our vantage in this business.

We'll over-reach the greybeard, Gremio,

The narrow-prying father, Minola,

The quaint musician, amorous Licio;

All for my master's sake, Lucentio.

Re-enter Gremio.

Signior Gremio, came you from the church?

GREMIO.

As willingly as e'er I came from school.

TRANIO.

And is the bride and bridegroom coming home?

GREMIO.

A bridegroom, say you? 'Tis a groom indeed,

A grumbling groom, and that the girl shall find.

TRANIO.

Curster than she? Why, 'tis impossible.

GREMIO.

Why, he's a devil, a devil, a very fiend.

TRANIO.

Why, she's a devil, a devil, the devil's dam.

GREMIO.

Tut! she's a lamb, a dove, a fool, to him.

I'll tell you, Sir Lucentio: when the priest

Should ask if Katherine should be his wife,

'Ay, by gogs-wouns' quoth he, and swore so loud

That, all amaz'd, the priest let fall the book;

And as he stoop'd again to take it up,

The mad-brain'd bridegroom took him such a cuff

That down fell priest and book, and book and priest:

'Now take them up,' quoth he 'if any list.'

TRANIO.

What said the wench, when he rose again?

GREMIO.

Trembled and shook, for why, he stamp'd and swore

As if the vicar meant to cozen him.

But after many ceremonies done,

He calls for wine: 'A health!' quoth he, as if

He had been abroad, carousing to his mates

After a storm; quaff'd off the muscadel,

And threw the sops all in the sexton's face,

Having no other reason

But that his beard grew thin and hungerly

And seem'd to ask him sops as he was drinking.

This done, he took the bride about the neck,

And kiss'd her lips with such a clamorous smack

That at the parting all the church did echo.

And I, seeing this, came thence for very shame;

And after me, I know, the rout is coming.

Such a mad marriage never was before.

Hark, hark! I hear the minstrels play.

[Music plays.]

Enter Petrucio, Katherina, Bianca, Baptista, Hortensio, Grumio and Train.

PETRUCHIO.

Gentlemen and friends, I thank you for your pains:

I know you think to dine with me today,

And have prepar'd great store of wedding cheer

But so it is, my haste doth call me hence,

And therefore here I mean to take my leave.

BAPTISTA.

Is't possible you will away tonight?

PETRUCHIO.

I must away today before night come.

Make it no wonder: if you knew my business,

You would entreat me rather go than stay.

And, honest company, I thank you all,

That have beheld me give away myself

To this most patient, sweet, and virtuous wife.

Dine with my father, drink a health to me.

For I must hence; and farewell to you all.

TRANIO.

Let us entreat you stay till after dinner.

PETRUCHIO.

It may not be.

GREMIO.

Let me entreat you.

PETRUCHIO.

It cannot be.

KATHERINA.

Let me entreat you.

PETRUCHIO.

I am content.

KATHERINA.

Are you content to stay?

PETRUCHIO.

I am content you shall entreat me stay;

But yet not stay, entreat me how you can.

KATHERINA.

Now, if you love me, stay.

PETRUCHIO.

Grumio, my horse!

GRUMIO.

Ay, sir, they be ready; the oats have eaten the horses.

KATHERINA.

Nay, then,

Do what thou canst, I will not go today;

No, nor tomorrow, not till I please myself.

The door is open, sir; there lies your way;

You may be jogging whiles your boots are green;

For me, I'll not be gone till I please myself.

'Tis like you'll prove a jolly surly groom

That take it on you at the first so roundly.

PETRUCHIO.

O Kate! content thee: prithee be not angry.

KATHERINA.

I will be angry: what hast thou to do?

Father, be quiet; he shall stay my leisure.

GREMIO.

Ay, marry, sir, now it begins to work.

KATHERINA.

Gentlemen, forward to the bridal dinner:

I see a woman may be made a fool,

If she had not a spirit to resist.

PETRUCHIO.

They shall go forward, Kate, at thy command.

Obey the bride, you that attend on her;

Go to the feast, revel and domineer,

Carouse full measure to her maidenhead,

Be mad and merry, or go hang yourselves:

But for my bonny Kate, she must with me.

Nay, look not big, nor stamp, nor stare, nor fret;

I will be master of what is mine own.

She is my goods, my chattels; she is my house,

My household stuff, my field, my barn,

My horse, my ox, my ass, my anything;

And here she stands, touch her whoever dare;

I'll bring mine action on the proudest he

That stops my way in Padua. Grumio,

Draw forth thy weapon; we are beset with thieves;

Rescue thy mistress, if thou be a man.

Fear not, sweet wench; they shall not touch thee, Kate;

I'll buckler thee against a million.

[Exeunt Petrucio, Katherina and Grumio.]

BAPTISTA.

Nay, let them go, a couple of quiet ones.

GREMIO.

Went they not quickly, I should die with laughing.

TRANIO.

Of all mad matches, never was the like.

LUCENTIO.

Mistress, what's your opinion of your sister?

BIANCA.

That, being mad herself, she's madly mated.

GREMIO.

I warrant him, Petruchio is Kated.

BAPTISTA.

Neighbours and friends, though bride and bridegroom wants

For to supply the places at the table,

You know there wants no junkets at the feast.

Lucentio, you shall supply the bridegroom's place;

And let Bianca take her sister's room.

TRANIO.

Shall sweet Bianca practise how to bride it?

BAPTISTA.

She shall, Lucentio. Come, gentlemen, let's go.

[Exeunt.]

ACT IV

SCENE I. A hall in PETRUCHIO'S country house.

Enter Grumio.

GRUMIO.

Fie, fie on all tired jades, on all mad masters, and all foul ways! Was ever man so beaten? Was ever man so ray'd? Was ever man so weary? I am sent before to make a fire, and they are coming after to warm them. Now, were not I a little pot and soon hot, my very lips might freeze to my teeth, my tongue to the roof of my mouth, my heart in my belly, ere I should come by a fire to thaw me. But I with blowing the fire shall warm myself; for, considering the weather, a taller man than I will take cold. Holla, ho! Curtis!

Enter Curtis.

CURTIS.

Who is that calls so coldly?

GRUMIO.

A piece of ice: if thou doubt it, thou mayst slide from my shoulder to my heel with no greater a run but my head and my neck. A fire, good Curtis.

CURTIS.

Is my master and his wife coming, Grumio?

GRUMIO.

O, ay! Curtis, ay; and therefore fire, fire; cast on no water.

CURTIS.

Is she so hot a shrew as she's reported?

GRUMIO.

She was, good Curtis, before this frost; but thou knowest winter tames man, woman, and beast; for it hath tamed my old master, and my new mistress, and myself, fellow Curtis.

CURTIS.

Away, you three-inch fool! I am no beast.

GRUMIO.

Am I but three inches? Why, thy horn is a foot; and so long am I at the least. But wilt thou make a fire, or shall I complain on thee to our mistress, whose hand,—she being now at hand,— thou shalt soon feel, to thy cold comfort, for being slow in thy hot office?

CURTIS.

I prithee, good Grumio, tell me, how goes the world?

GRUMIO.

A cold world, Curtis, in every office but thine; and therefore fire. Do thy duty, and have thy duty, for my master and mistress are almost frozen to death.

CURTIS.

There's fire ready; and therefore, good Grumio, the news.

GRUMIO.

Why, 'Jack boy! ho, boy!' and as much news as wilt thou.

CURTIS.

Come, you are so full of cony-catching.

GRUMIO.

Why, therefore, fire; for I have caught extreme cold. Where's the cook? Is supper ready, the house trimmed, rushes strewed, cobwebs swept, the servingmen in their new fustian, their white stockings, and every officer his wedding-garment on? Be the Jacks fair within, the Jills fair without, and carpets laid, and everything in order?

CURTIS.

All ready; and therefore, I pray thee, news.

GRUMIO.

First, know my horse is tired; my master and mistress fallen out.

CURTIS.

How?

GRUMIO.

Out of their saddles into the dirt; and thereby hangs a tale.

CURTIS.

Let's ha't, good Grumio.

GRUMIO.

Lend thine ear.

CURTIS.

Here.

GRUMIO.

[Striking him.] There.

CURTIS.

This 'tis to feel a tale, not to hear a tale.

GRUMIO.

And therefore 'tis called a sensible tale; and this cuff was but to knock at your ear and beseech listening. Now I begin: Imprimis, we came down a foul hill, my master riding behind my mistress,—

CURTIS.

Both of one horse?

GRUMIO.

What's that to thee?

CURTIS.

Why, a horse.

GRUMIO.

Tell thou the tale: but hadst thou not crossed me, thou shouldst have heard how her horse fell, and she under her horse; thou shouldst have heard in how miry a place, how she was bemoiled; how he left her with the horse upon her; how he beat me because her horse stumbled; how she waded through the dirt to pluck him off me: how he swore; how she prayed, that never prayed before; how I cried; how the horses ran away; how her bridle was burst; how I lost my crupper; with many things of worthy memory, which now shall die in oblivion, and thou return unexperienced to thy grave.

CURTIS.

By this reckoning he is more shrew than she.

GRUMIO.

Ay; and that thou and the proudest of you all shall find when he comes home. But what talk I of this? Call forth Nathaniel, Joseph, Nicholas, Philip, Walter, Sugarsop, and the rest; let their heads be sleekly combed, their blue coats brush'd and their garters of an indifferent knit; let them curtsy with their left legs, and not presume to touch a hair of my master's horse-tail till they kiss their hands. Are they all ready?

CURTIS.

They are.

GRUMIO.

Call them forth.

CURTIS.

Do you hear? ho! You must meet my master to countenance my mistress.

GRUMIO.

Why, she hath a face of her own.

CURTIS.

Who knows not that?

GRUMIO.

Thou, it seems, that calls for company to countenance her.

CURTIS.

I call them forth to credit her.

GRUMIO.

Why, she comes to borrow nothing of them.

Enter four or five Servants.

NATHANIEL.

Welcome home, Grumio!

PHILIP.

How now, Grumio!

JOSEPH.

What, Grumio!

NICHOLAS.

Fellow Grumio!

NATHANIEL.

How now, old lad!

GRUMIO.

Welcome, you; how now, you; what, you; fellow, you; and thus much for greeting. Now, my spruce companions, is all ready, and all things neat?

NATHANIEL.

All things is ready. How near is our master?

GRUMIO.

E'en at hand, alighted by this; and therefore be not,—

Cock's passion, silence! I hear my master.

Enter Petrucio and Katherina.

PETRUCHIO.

Where be these knaves? What! no man at door

To hold my stirrup nor to take my horse?

Where is Nathaniel, Gregory, Philip?—

ALL SERVANTS.

Here, here, sir; here, sir.

PETRUCHIO.

Here, sir! here, sir! here, sir! here, sir!

You logger-headed and unpolish'd grooms!

What, no attendance? no regard? no duty?

Where is the foolish knave I sent before?

GRUMIO.

Here, sir; as foolish as I was before.

PETRUCHIO.

You peasant swain! you whoreson malt-horse drudge!

Did I not bid thee meet me in the park,

And bring along these rascal knaves with thee?

GRUMIO.

Nathaniel's coat, sir, was not fully made,

And Gabriel's pumps were all unpink'd i' the heel;

There was no link to colour Peter's hat,

And Walter's dagger was not come from sheathing;

There was none fine but Adam, Ralph, and Gregory;

The rest were ragged, old, and beggarly;

Yet, as they are, here are they come to meet you.

PETRUCHIO.

Go, rascals, go and fetch my supper in.

[Exeunt some of the Servants.]

Where is the life that late I led?

Where are those—? Sit down, Kate, and welcome.

Food, food, food, food!

Re-enter Servants with supper.

Why, when, I say?—Nay, good sweet Kate, be merry.—

Off with my boots, you rogues! you villains! when?

It was the friar of orders grey,

As he forth walked on his way:

Out, you rogue! you pluck my foot awry:

[Strikes him.]

Take that, and mend the plucking off the other.

Be merry, Kate. Some water, here; what, ho!

Where's my spaniel Troilus? Sirrah, get you hence

And bid my cousin Ferdinand come hither:

[Exit Servant.]

One, Kate, that you must kiss and be acquainted with.

Where are my slippers? Shall I have some water?

Come, Kate, and wash, and welcome heartily.—

[Servant lets the ewer fall. Petruchio strikes him.]

You whoreson villain! will you let it fall?

KATHERINA.

Patience, I pray you; 'twas a fault unwilling.

PETRUCHIO.

A whoreson, beetle-headed, flap-ear'd knave!

Come, Kate, sit down; I know you have a stomach.

Will you give thanks, sweet Kate, or else shall I?—

What's this? Mutton?

FIRST SERVANT.

Ay.

PETRUCHIO.

Who brought it?

PETER.

I.

PETRUCHIO.

'Tis burnt; and so is all the meat.

What dogs are these! Where is the rascal cook?

How durst you, villains, bring it from the dresser,

And serve it thus to me that love it not?

[Throws the meat, etc., at them.]

There, take it to you, trenchers, cups, and all.

You heedless joltheads and unmanner'd slaves!

What! do you grumble? I'll be with you straight.

KATHERINA.

I pray you, husband, be not so disquiet;

The meat was well, if you were so contented.

PETRUCHIO.

I tell thee, Kate, 'twas burnt and dried away,

And I expressly am forbid to touch it;

For it engenders choler, planteth anger;

And better 'twere that both of us did fast,

Since, of ourselves, ourselves are choleric,

Than feed it with such over-roasted flesh.

Be patient; tomorrow 't shall be mended.

And for this night we'll fast for company:

Come, I will bring thee to thy bridal chamber.

[Exeunt Petruchio, Katherina and Curtis.]

NATHANIEL.

Peter, didst ever see the like?

PETER.

He kills her in her own humour.

Re-enter Curtis.

GRUMIO.

Where is he?

CURTIS.

In her chamber, making a sermon of continency to her;

And rails, and swears, and rates, that she, poor soul,

Knows not which way to stand, to look, to speak,

And sits as one new risen from a dream.

Away, away! for he is coming hither.

[Exeunt.]

Re-enter Petruchio.

PETRUCHIO.

Thus have I politicly begun my reign,

And 'tis my hope to end successfully.

My falcon now is sharp and passing empty.

And till she stoop she must not be full-gorg'd,

For then she never looks upon her lure.

Another way I have to man my haggard,

To make her come, and know her keeper's call,

That is, to watch her, as we watch these kites

That bate and beat, and will not be obedient.

She eat no meat today, nor none shall eat;

Last night she slept not, nor tonight she shall not;

As with the meat, some undeserved fault

I'll find about the making of the bed;

And here I'll fling the pillow, there the bolster,

This way the coverlet, another way the sheets;

Ay, and amid this hurly I intend

That all is done in reverend care of her;

And, in conclusion, she shall watch all night:

And if she chance to nod I'll rail and brawl,

And with the clamour keep her still awake.

This is a way to kill a wife with kindness;

And thus I'll curb her mad and headstrong humour.

He that knows better how to tame a shrew,

Now let him speak; 'tis charity to show.

[Exit.]

SCENE II. Padua. Before BAPTISTA'S house.

Enter Tranio and Hortensio.

TRANIO.

Is 't possible, friend Licio, that Mistress Bianca

Doth fancy any other but Lucentio?

I tell you, sir, she bears me fair in hand.

HORTENSIO.

Sir, to satisfy you in what I have said,

Stand by and mark the manner of his teaching.

[They stand aside.]

Enter Bianca and Lucentio.

LUCENTIO.

Now, mistress, profit you in what you read?

BIANCA.

What, master, read you? First resolve me that.

LUCENTIO.

I read that I profess, The Art to Love.

BIANCA.

And may you prove, sir, master of your art!

LUCENTIO.

While you, sweet dear, prove mistress of my heart.

[They retire.]

HORTENSIO.

Quick proceeders, marry! Now tell me, I pray,

You that durst swear that your Mistress Bianca

Lov'd none in the world so well as Lucentio.

TRANIO.

O despiteful love! unconstant womankind!

I tell thee, Licio, this is wonderful.

HORTENSIO.

Mistake no more; I am not Licio.

Nor a musician as I seem to be;

But one that scorn to live in this disguise

For such a one as leaves a gentleman

And makes a god of such a cullion:

Know, sir, that I am call'd Hortensio.

TRANIO.

Signior Hortensio, I have often heard

Of your entire affection to Bianca;

And since mine eyes are witness of her lightness,

I will with you, if you be so contented,

Forswear Bianca and her love for ever.

HORTENSIO.

See, how they kiss and court! Signior Lucentio,

Here is my hand, and here I firmly vow

Never to woo her more, but do forswear her,

As one unworthy all the former favours

That I have fondly flatter'd her withal.

TRANIO.

And here I take the like unfeigned oath,

Never to marry with her though she would entreat;

Fie on her! See how beastly she doth court him!

HORTENSIO.

Would all the world but he had quite forsworn!

For me, that I may surely keep mine oath,

I will be married to a wealthy widow

Ere three days pass, which hath as long lov'd me

As I have lov'd this proud disdainful haggard.

And so farewell, Signior Lucentio.

Kindness in women, not their beauteous looks,

Shall win my love; and so I take my leave,

In resolution as I swore before.

> [Exit Hortensio. Lucentio and Bianca advance.]

TRANIO.

Mistress Bianca, bless you with such grace

As 'longeth to a lover's blessed case!

Nay, I have ta'en you napping, gentle love,

And have forsworn you with Hortensio.

BIANCA.

Tranio, you jest; but have you both forsworn me?

TRANIO.

Mistress, we have.

LUCENTIO.

Then we are rid of Licio.

TRANIO.

I' faith, he'll have a lusty widow now,

That shall be woo'd and wedded in a day.

BIANCA.

God give him joy!

TRANIO.

Ay, and he'll tame her.

BIANCA.

He says so, Tranio.

TRANIO.

Faith, he is gone unto the taming-school.

BIANCA.

The taming-school! What, is there such a place?

TRANIO.

Ay, mistress; and Petruchio is the master,

That teacheth tricks eleven and twenty long,

To tame a shrew and charm her chattering tongue.

Enter Biondello, running.

BIONDELLO.

O master, master! I have watch'd so long

That I am dog-weary; but at last I spied

An ancient angel coming down the hill

Will serve the turn.

TRANIO.

What is he, Biondello?

BIONDELLO.

Master, a mercatante or a pedant,

I know not what; but formal in apparel,

In gait and countenance surely like a father.

LUCENTIO.

And what of him, Tranio?

TRANIO.

If he be credulous and trust my tale,

I'll make him glad to seem Vincentio,

And give assurance to Baptista Minola,

As if he were the right Vincentio.

Take in your love, and then let me alone.

[Exeunt Lucentio and Bianca.]

Enter a Pedant.

PEDANT.

God save you, sir!

TRANIO.

And you, sir! you are welcome.

Travel you far on, or are you at the farthest?

PEDANT.

Sir, at the farthest for a week or two;

But then up farther, and as far as Rome;

And so to Tripoli, if God lend me life.

TRANIO.

What countryman, I pray?

PEDANT.

Of Mantua.

TRANIO.

Of Mantua, sir? Marry, God forbid,

And come to Padua, careless of your life!

PEDANT.

My life, sir! How, I pray? for that goes hard.

TRANIO.

'Tis death for anyone in Mantua

To come to Padua. Know you not the cause?

Your ships are stay'd at Venice; and the Duke,—

For private quarrel 'twixt your Duke and him,—

Hath publish'd and proclaim'd it openly.

'Tis marvel, but that you are but newly come

You might have heard it else proclaim'd about.

PEDANT.

Alas, sir! it is worse for me than so;

For I have bills for money by exchange

From Florence, and must here deliver them.

TRANIO.

Well, sir, to do you courtesy,

This will I do, and this I will advise you:

First, tell me, have you ever been at Pisa?

PEDANT.

Ay, sir, in Pisa have I often been,

Pisa renowned for grave citizens.

TRANIO.

Among them know you one Vincentio?

PEDANT.

I know him not, but I have heard of him,

A merchant of incomparable wealth.

TRANIO.

He is my father, sir; and, sooth to say,

In countenance somewhat doth resemble you.

BIONDELLO.

[Aside.] As much as an apple doth an oyster, and all one.

TRANIO.

To save your life in this extremity,

This favour will I do you for his sake;

And think it not the worst of all your fortunes

That you are like to Sir Vincentio.

His name and credit shall you undertake,

And in my house you shall be friendly lodg'd;

Look that you take upon you as you should!

You understand me, sir; so shall you stay

Till you have done your business in the city.

If this be courtesy, sir, accept of it.

PEDANT.

O, sir, I do; and will repute you ever

The patron of my life and liberty.

TRANIO.

Then go with me to make the matter good.

This, by the way, I let you understand:

My father is here look'd for every day

To pass assurance of a dower in marriage

'Twixt me and one Baptista's daughter here:

In all these circumstances I'll instruct you.

Go with me to clothe you as becomes you.

[Exeunt.]

SCENE III. A room in PETRUCHIO'S house.

Enter Katherina and Grumio.

GRUMIO.

No, no, forsooth; I dare not for my life.

KATHERINA.

The more my wrong, the more his spite appears.

What, did he marry me to famish me?

Beggars that come unto my father's door

Upon entreaty have a present alms;

If not, elsewhere they meet with charity;

But I, who never knew how to entreat,

Nor never needed that I should entreat,

Am starv'd for meat, giddy for lack of sleep;

With oaths kept waking, and with brawling fed.

And that which spites me more than all these wants,

He does it under name of perfect love;

As who should say, if I should sleep or eat

'Twere deadly sickness, or else present death.

I prithee go and get me some repast;

I care not what, so it be wholesome food.

GRUMIO.

What say you to a neat's foot?

KATHERINA.

'Tis passing good; I prithee let me have it.

GRUMIO.

I fear it is too choleric a meat.

How say you to a fat tripe finely broil'd?

KATHERINA.

I like it well; good Grumio, fetch it me.

GRUMIO.

I cannot tell; I fear 'tis choleric.

What say you to a piece of beef and mustard?

KATHERINA.

A dish that I do love to feed upon.

GRUMIO.

Ay, but the mustard is too hot a little.

KATHERINA.

Why then the beef, and let the mustard rest.

GRUMIO.

Nay, then I will not: you shall have the mustard,

Or else you get no beef of Grumio.

KATHERINA.

Then both, or one, or anything thou wilt.

GRUMIO.

Why then the mustard without the beef.

KATHERINA.

Go, get thee gone, thou false deluding slave,

[Beats him.]

That feed'st me with the very name of meat.

Sorrow on thee and all the pack of you

That triumph thus upon my misery!

Go, get thee gone, I say.

Enter Petruchio with a dish of meat; and Hortensio.

PETRUCHIO.

How fares my Kate? What, sweeting, all amort?

HORTENSIO.

Mistress, what cheer?

KATHERINA.

Faith, as cold as can be.

PETRUCHIO.

Pluck up thy spirits; look cheerfully upon me.

Here, love; thou seest how diligent I am,

To dress thy meat myself, and bring it thee:

[Sets the dish on a table.]

I am sure, sweet Kate, this kindness merits thanks.

What! not a word? Nay, then thou lov'st it not,

And all my pains is sorted to no proof.

Here, take away this dish.

KATHERINA.

I pray you, let it stand.

PETRUCHIO.

The poorest service is repaid with thanks;

And so shall mine, before you touch the meat.

KATHERINA.

I thank you, sir.

HORTENSIO.

Signior Petruchio, fie! you are to blame.

Come, Mistress Kate, I'll bear you company.

PETRUCHIO.

[Aside.] Eat it up all, Hortensio, if thou lovest me.

Much good do it unto thy gentle heart!

Kate, eat apace: and now, my honey love,

Will we return unto thy father's house

And revel it as bravely as the best,

With silken coats and caps, and golden rings,

With ruffs and cuffs and farthingales and things;

With scarfs and fans and double change of bravery,

With amber bracelets, beads, and all this knavery.

What! hast thou din'd? The tailor stays thy leisure,

To deck thy body with his ruffling treasure.

Enter Tailor.

Come, tailor, let us see these ornaments;

Lay forth the gown.—

Enter Haberdasher.

What news with you, sir?

HABERDASHER.

Here is the cap your worship did bespeak.

PETRUCHIO.

Why, this was moulded on a porringer;

A velvet dish: fie, fie! 'tis lewd and filthy:

Why, 'tis a cockle or a walnut-shell,

A knack, a toy, a trick, a baby's cap:

Away with it! come, let me have a bigger.

KATHERINA.

I'll have no bigger; this doth fit the time,

And gentlewomen wear such caps as these.

PETRUCHIO.

When you are gentle, you shall have one too,

And not till then.

HORTENSIO.

[Aside] That will not be in haste.

KATHERINA.

Why, sir, I trust I may have leave to speak;

And speak I will. I am no child, no babe.

Your betters have endur'd me say my mind,

And if you cannot, best you stop your ears.

My tongue will tell the anger of my heart,

Or else my heart, concealing it, will break;

And rather than it shall, I will be free

Even to the uttermost, as I please, in words.

PETRUCHIO.

Why, thou say'st true; it is a paltry cap,

A custard-coffin, a bauble, a silken pie;

I love thee well in that thou lik'st it not.

KATHERINA.

Love me or love me not, I like the cap;

And it I will have, or I will have none.

[Exit Haberdasher.]

PETRUCHIO.

Thy gown? Why, ay: come, tailor, let us see't.

O mercy, God! what masquing stuff is here?

What's this? A sleeve? 'Tis like a demi-cannon.

What, up and down, carv'd like an apple tart?

Here's snip and nip and cut and slish and slash,

Like to a censer in a barber's shop.

Why, what i' devil's name, tailor, call'st thou this?

HORTENSIO.

[Aside] I see she's like to have neither cap nor gown.

TAILOR.

You bid me make it orderly and well,

According to the fashion and the time.

PETRUCHIO.

Marry, and did; but if you be remember'd,

I did not bid you mar it to the time.

Go, hop me over every kennel home,

For you shall hop without my custom, sir.

I'll none of it: hence! make your best of it.

KATHERINA.

I never saw a better fashion'd gown,

More quaint, more pleasing, nor more commendable;

Belike you mean to make a puppet of me.

PETRUCHIO.

Why, true; he means to make a puppet of thee.

TAILOR.

She says your worship means to make a puppet of her.

PETRUCHIO.

O monstrous arrogance! Thou liest, thou thread,

Thou thimble,

Thou yard, three-quarters, half-yard, quarter, nail!

Thou flea, thou nit, thou winter-cricket thou!

Brav'd in mine own house with a skein of thread!

Away! thou rag, thou quantity, thou remnant,

Or I shall so be-mete thee with thy yard

As thou shalt think on prating whilst thou liv'st!

I tell thee, I, that thou hast marr'd her gown.

TAILOR.

Your worship is deceiv'd: the gown is made

Just as my master had direction.

Grumio gave order how it should be done.

GRUMIO.

I gave him no order; I gave him the stuff.

TAILOR.

But how did you desire it should be made?

GRUMIO.

Marry, sir, with needle and thread.

TAILOR.

But did you not request to have it cut?

GRUMIO.

Thou hast faced many things.

TAILOR.

I have.

GRUMIO.

Face not me. Thou hast braved many men; brave not me: I will neither be fac'd nor brav'd. I say unto thee, I bid thy master cut out the gown; but I did not bid him cut it to pieces: ergo, thou liest.

TAILOR.

Why, here is the note of the fashion to testify.

PETRUCHIO.

Read it.

GRUMIO.

The note lies in 's throat, if he say I said so.

TAILOR.

'Imprimis, a loose-bodied gown.'

GRUMIO.

Master, if ever I said loose-bodied gown, sew me in the skirts of it and beat me to death with a bottom of brown thread; I said, a gown.

PETRUCHIO.

Proceed.

TAILOR.

'With a small compassed cape.'

GRUMIO.

I confess the cape.

TAILOR.

'With a trunk sleeve.'

GRUMIO.

I confess two sleeves.

TAILOR.

'The sleeves curiously cut.'

PETRUCHIO.

Ay, there's the villainy.

GRUMIO.

Error i' the bill, sir; error i' the bill. I commanded the sleeves should be cut out, and sew'd up again; and that I'll prove upon thee, though thy little finger be armed in a thimble.

TAILOR.

This is true that I say; and I had thee in place where thou shouldst know it.

GRUMIO.

I am for thee straight; take thou the bill, give me thy mete-yard, and spare not me.

HORTENSIO.

God-a-mercy, Grumio! Then he shall have no odds.

PETRUCHIO.

Well, sir, in brief, the gown is not for me.

GRUMIO.

You are i' the right, sir; 'tis for my mistress.

PETRUCHIO.

Go, take it up unto thy master's use.

GRUMIO.

Villain, not for thy life! Take up my mistress' gown for thy master's use!

PETRUCHIO.

Why, sir, what's your conceit in that?

GRUMIO.

O, sir, the conceit is deeper than you think for.

Take up my mistress' gown to his master's use!

O fie, fie, fie!

PETRUCHIO.

[Aside] Hortensio, say thou wilt see the tailor paid.

[To Tailor.] Go take it hence; be gone, and say no more.

HORTENSIO.

[Aside to Tailor.] Tailor, I'll pay thee for thy gown tomorrow;

Take no unkindness of his hasty words.

Away, I say! commend me to thy master.

[Exit Tailor.]

PETRUCHIO.

Well, come, my Kate; we will unto your father's

Even in these honest mean habiliments.

Our purses shall be proud, our garments poor

For 'tis the mind that makes the body rich;

And as the sun breaks through the darkest clouds,

So honour peereth in the meanest habit.

What, is the jay more precious than the lark

Because his feathers are more beautiful?

Or is the adder better than the eel

Because his painted skin contents the eye?

O no, good Kate; neither art thou the worse

For this poor furniture and mean array.

If thou account'st it shame, lay it on me;

And therefore frolic; we will hence forthwith,

To feast and sport us at thy father's house.

Go call my men, and let us straight to him;

And bring our horses unto Long-lane end;

There will we mount, and thither walk on foot.

Let's see; I think 'tis now some seven o'clock,

And well we may come there by dinner-time.

KATHERINA.

I dare assure you, sir, 'tis almost two,

And 'twill be supper-time ere you come there.

PETRUCHIO.

It shall be seven ere I go to horse.

Look what I speak, or do, or think to do,

You are still crossing it. Sirs, let 't alone:

I will not go today; and ere I do,

It shall be what o'clock I say it is.

HORTENSIO.

Why, so this gallant will command the sun.

[Exeunt.]

SCENE IV. Padua. Before BAPTISTA'S house.

Enter Tranio and the Pedant dressed like Vincentio

TRANIO.

Sir, this is the house; please it you that I call?

PEDANT.

Ay, what else? and, but I be deceived,

Signior Baptista may remember me,

Near twenty years ago in Genoa,

Where we were lodgers at the Pegasus.

TRANIO.

'Tis well; and hold your own, in any case,

With such austerity as 'longeth to a father.

PEDANT.

I warrant you. But, sir, here comes your boy;

'Twere good he were school'd.

Enter Biondello.

TRANIO.

Fear you not him. Sirrah Biondello,

Now do your duty throughly, I advise you.

Imagine 'twere the right Vincentio.

BIONDELLO.

Tut! fear not me.

TRANIO.

But hast thou done thy errand to Baptista?

BIONDELLO.

I told him that your father was at Venice,

And that you look'd for him this day in Padua.

TRANIO.

Th'art a tall fellow; hold thee that to drink.

Here comes Baptista. Set your countenance, sir.

Enter Baptista and Lucentio.

Signior Baptista, you are happily met.

[To the Pedant] Sir, this is the gentleman I told you of;

I pray you stand good father to me now;

Give me Bianca for my patrimony.

PEDANT.

Soft, son!

Sir, by your leave: having come to Padua

To gather in some debts, my son Lucentio

Made me acquainted with a weighty cause

Of love between your daughter and himself:

And,—for the good report I hear of you,

And for the love he beareth to your daughter,

And she to him,—to stay him not too long,

I am content, in a good father's care,

To have him match'd; and, if you please to like

No worse than I, upon some agreement

Me shall you find ready and willing

With one consent to have her so bestow'd;

For curious I cannot be with you,

Signior Baptista, of whom I hear so well.

BAPTISTA.

Sir, pardon me in what I have to say.

Your plainness and your shortness please me well.

Right true it is your son Lucentio here

Doth love my daughter, and she loveth him,

Or both dissemble deeply their affections;

And therefore, if you say no more than this,

That like a father you will deal with him,

And pass my daughter a sufficient dower,

The match is made, and all is done:

Your son shall have my daughter with consent.

TRANIO.

I thank you, sir. Where then do you know best

We be affied, and such assurance ta'en

As shall with either part's agreement stand?

BAPTISTA.

Not in my house, Lucentio, for you know

Pitchers have ears, and I have many servants;

Besides, old Gremio is hearkening still,

And happily we might be interrupted.

TRANIO.

Then at my lodging, and it like you:

There doth my father lie; and there this night

We'll pass the business privately and well.

Send for your daughter by your servant here;

My boy shall fetch the scrivener presently.

The worst is this, that at so slender warning

You are like to have a thin and slender pittance.

BAPTISTA.

It likes me well. Cambio, hie you home,

And bid Bianca make her ready straight;

And, if you will, tell what hath happened:

Lucentio's father is arriv'd in Padua,

And how she's like to be Lucentio's wife.

LUCENTIO.

I pray the gods she may, with all my heart!

TRANIO.

Dally not with the gods, but get thee gone.

Signior Baptista, shall I lead the way?

Welcome! One mess is like to be your cheer;

Come, sir; we will better it in Pisa.

BAPTISTA.

I follow you.

[Exeunt Tranio, Pedant and Baptista.]

BIONDELLO.

Cambio!

LUCENTIO.

What say'st thou, Biondello?

BIONDELLO.

You saw my master wink and laugh upon you?

LUCENTIO.

Biondello, what of that?

BIONDELLO.

Faith, nothing; but has left me here behind to expound the meaning or moral of his signs and tokens.

LUCENTIO.

I pray thee moralize them.

BIONDELLO.

Then thus: Baptista is safe, talking with the deceiving father of a deceitful son.

LUCENTIO.

And what of him?

BIONDELLO.

His daughter is to be brought by you to the supper.

LUCENTIO.

And then?

BIONDELLO.

The old priest at Saint Luke's church is at your command at all hours.

LUCENTIO.

And what of all this?

BIONDELLO.

I cannot tell, except they are busied about a counterfeit assurance. Take your assurance of her, cum privilegio ad imprimendum solum; to the church! take the priest, clerk, and some sufficient honest witnesses.

If this be not that you look for, I have more to say,

But bid Bianca farewell for ever and a day.

[Going.]

LUCENTIO.

Hear'st thou, Biondello?

BIONDELLO.

I cannot tarry: I knew a wench married in an afternoon as she went to the garden for parsley to stuff a rabbit; and so may you, sir; and so adieu, sir. My master hath appointed me to go to Saint Luke's to bid the priest be ready to come against you come with your appendix.

[Exit.]

LUCENTIO.

I may, and will, if she be so contented.

She will be pleas'd; then wherefore should I doubt?

Hap what hap may, I'll roundly go about her;

It shall go hard if Cambio go without her:

[Exit.]

SCENE V. A public road.

Enter Petruchio, Katherina, Hortensio and Servants.

PETRUCHIO.

Come on, i' God's name; once more toward our father's.

Good Lord, how bright and goodly shines the moon!

KATHERINA.

The moon! The sun; it is not moonlight now.

PETRUCHIO.

I say it is the moon that shines so bright.

KATHERINA.

I know it is the sun that shines so bright.

PETRUCHIO.

Now by my mother's son, and that's myself,

It shall be moon, or star, or what I list,

Or ere I journey to your father's house.

Go on and fetch our horses back again.

Evermore cross'd and cross'd; nothing but cross'd!

HORTENSIO.

Say as he says, or we shall never go.

KATHERINA.

Forward, I pray, since we have come so far,

And be it moon, or sun, or what you please;

And if you please to call it a rush-candle,

Henceforth I vow it shall be so for me.

PETRUCHIO.

I say it is the moon.

KATHERINA.

I know it is the moon.

PETRUCHIO.

Nay, then you lie; it is the blessed sun.

KATHERINA.

Then, God be bless'd, it is the blessed sun;

But sun it is not when you say it is not,

And the moon changes even as your mind.

What you will have it nam'd, even that it is,

And so it shall be so for Katherine.

HORTENSIO.

Petruchio, go thy ways; the field is won.

PETRUCHIO.

Well, forward, forward! thus the bowl should run,

And not unluckily against the bias.

But, soft! Company is coming here.

Enter Vincentio, in a travelling dress.

[To Vincentio] Good morrow, gentle mistress; where away?

Tell me, sweet Kate, and tell me truly too,

Hast thou beheld a fresher gentlewoman?

Such war of white and red within her cheeks!

What stars do spangle heaven with such beauty

As those two eyes become that heavenly face?

Fair lovely maid, once more good day to thee.

Sweet Kate, embrace her for her beauty's sake.

HORTENSIO.

A will make the man mad, to make a woman of him.

KATHERINA.

Young budding virgin, fair and fresh and sweet,

Whither away, or where is thy abode?

Happy the parents of so fair a child;

Happier the man whom favourable stars

Allot thee for his lovely bedfellow.

PETRUCHIO.

Why, how now, Kate! I hope thou art not mad:

This is a man, old, wrinkled, faded, wither'd,

And not a maiden, as thou sayst he is.

KATHERINA.

Pardon, old father, my mistaking eyes,

That have been so bedazzled with the sun

That everything I look on seemeth green:

Now I perceive thou art a reverend father;

Pardon, I pray thee, for my mad mistaking.

PETRUCHIO.

Do, good old grandsire, and withal make known

Which way thou travellest: if along with us,

We shall be joyful of thy company.

VINCENTIO.

Fair sir, and you my merry mistress,

That with your strange encounter much amaz'd me,

My name is called Vincentio; my dwelling Pisa;

And bound I am to Padua, there to visit

A son of mine, which long I have not seen.

PETRUCHIO.

What is his name?

VINCENTIO.

Lucentio, gentle sir.

PETRUCHIO.

Happily met; the happier for thy son.

And now by law, as well as reverend age,

I may entitle thee my loving father:

The sister to my wife, this gentlewoman,

Thy son by this hath married. Wonder not,

Nor be not griev'd: she is of good esteem,

Her dowry wealthy, and of worthy birth;

Beside, so qualified as may beseem

The spouse of any noble gentleman.

Let me embrace with old Vincentio;

And wander we to see thy honest son,

Who will of thy arrival be full joyous.

VINCENTIO.

But is this true? or is it else your pleasure,

Like pleasant travellers, to break a jest

Upon the company you overtake?

HORTENSIO.

I do assure thee, father, so it is.

PETRUCHIO.

Come, go along, and see the truth hereof;

For our first merriment hath made thee jealous.

[Exeunt all but Hortensio.]

HORTENSIO.

Well, Petruchio, this has put me in heart.

Have to my widow! and if she be froward,

Then hast thou taught Hortensio to be untoward.

[Exit.]

ACT V

SCENE I. Padua. Before LUCENTIO'S house.

Enter on one side Biondello, Lucentio and Bianca; Gremio walking on other side.

BIONDELLO.

Softly and swiftly, sir, for the priest is ready.

LUCENTIO.

I fly, Biondello; but they may chance to need thee at home, therefore leave us.

BIONDELLO.

Nay, faith, I'll see the church o' your back; and then come back to my master's as soon as I can.

[Exeunt Lucentio, Bianca and Biondello.]

GREMIO.

I marvel Cambio comes not all this while.

Enter Petruchio, Katherina, Vincentio and Attendants.

PETRUCHIO.

Sir, here's the door; this is Lucentio's house:

My father's bears more toward the market-place;

Thither must I, and here I leave you, sir.

VINCENTIO.

You shall not choose but drink before you go.

I think I shall command your welcome here,

And by all likelihood some cheer is toward.

[Knocks.]

GREMIO.

They're busy within; you were best knock louder.

Enter Pedant above, at a window.

PEDANT.

What's he that knocks as he would beat down the gate?

VINCENTIO.

Is Signior Lucentio within, sir?

PEDANT.

He's within, sir, but not to be spoken withal.

VINCENTIO.

What if a man bring him a hundred pound or two to make merry withal?

PEDANT.

Keep your hundred pounds to yourself: he shall need none so long as I live.

PETRUCHIO.

Nay, I told you your son was well beloved in Padua. Do you hear, sir? To leave frivolous circumstances, I pray you tell Signior Lucentio that his father is come from Pisa, and is here at the door to speak with him.

PEDANT.

Thou liest: his father is come from Padua, and here looking out at the window.

VINCENTIO.

Art thou his father?

PEDANT.

Ay, sir; so his mother says, if I may believe her.

PETRUCHIO.

[To Vincentio] Why, how now, gentleman! why, this is flat knavery to take upon you another man's name.

PEDANT.

Lay hands on the villain: I believe a means to cozen somebody in this city under my countenance.

Re-enter Biondello.

BIONDELLO.

I have seen them in the church together: God send 'em good shipping! But who is here? Mine old master, Vincentio! Now we are undone and brought to nothing.

VINCENTIO.

[Seeing Biondello.] Come hither, crack-hemp.

BIONDELLO.

I hope I may choose, sir.

VINCENTIO.

Come hither, you rogue. What, have you forgot me?

BIONDELLO.

Forgot you! No, sir: I could not forget you, for I never saw you before in all my life.

VINCENTIO.

What, you notorious villain! didst thou never see thy master's father,

Vincentio?

BIONDELLO.

What, my old worshipful old master? Yes, marry, sir; see where he looks out of the window.

VINCENTIO.

Is't so, indeed?

[He beats Biondello.]

BIONDELLO.

Help, help, help! here's a madman will murder me.

[Exit.]

PEDANT.

Help, son! help, Signior Baptista!

[Exit from the window.]

PETRUCHIO.

Prithee, Kate, let's stand aside and see the end of this controversy.

[They retire.]

Re-enter Pedant, below; Baptista, Tranio and Servants.

TRANIO.

Sir, what are you that offer to beat my servant?

VINCENTIO.

What am I, sir! nay, what are you, sir? O immortal gods! O fine villain! A silken doublet, a velvet hose, a scarlet cloak, and a copatain hat! O, I am undone! I am undone! While I play the good husband at home, my son and my servant spend all at the university.

TRANIO.

How now! what's the matter?

BAPTISTA.

What, is the man lunatic?

TRANIO.

Sir, you seem a sober ancient gentleman by your habit, but your words show you a madman. Why, sir, what 'cerns it you if I wear pearl and gold? I thank my good father, I am able to maintain it.

VINCENTIO.

Thy father! O villain! he is a sailmaker in Bergamo.

BAPTISTA.

You mistake, sir; you mistake, sir. Pray, what do you think is his name?

VINCENTIO.

His name! As if I knew not his name! I have brought him up ever since he was three years old, and his name is Tranio.

PEDANT.

Away, away, mad ass! His name is Lucentio; and he is mine only son, and heir to the lands of me, Signior Vincentio.

VINCENTIO.

Lucentio! O, he hath murdered his master! Lay hold on him, I charge you, in the Duke's name. O, my son, my son! Tell me, thou villain, where is my son, Lucentio?

TRANIO.

Call forth an officer.

Enter one with an Officer.

Carry this mad knave to the gaol. Father Baptista, I charge you see that he be forthcoming.

VINCENTIO.

Carry me to the gaol!

GREMIO.

Stay, officer; he shall not go to prison.

BAPTISTA.

Talk not, Signior Gremio; I say he shall go to prison.

GREMIO.

Take heed, Signior Baptista, lest you be cony-catched in this business; I dare swear this is the right Vincentio.

PEDANT.

Swear if thou darest.

GREMIO.

Nay, I dare not swear it.

TRANIO.

Then thou wert best say that I am not Lucentio.

GREMIO.

Yes, I know thee to be Signior Lucentio.

BAPTISTA.

Away with the dotard! to the gaol with him!

VINCENTIO.

Thus strangers may be haled and abus'd: O monstrous villain!

Re-enter Biondello, with Lucentio and Bianca.

BIONDELLO.

O! we are spoiled; and yonder he is: deny him, forswear him, or else we are all undone.

LUCENTIO.

[Kneeling.] Pardon, sweet father.

VINCENTIO.

Lives my sweetest son?

                            [Biondello, Tranio and Pedant run out.]

BIANCA.

[Kneeling.] Pardon, dear father.

BAPTISTA.

How hast thou offended?

Where is Lucentio?

LUCENTIO.

Here's Lucentio,

Right son to the right Vincentio;

That have by marriage made thy daughter mine,

While counterfeit supposes blear'd thine eyne.

GREMIO.

Here 's packing, with a witness, to deceive us all!

VINCENTIO.

Where is that damned villain, Tranio,

That fac'd and brav'd me in this matter so?

BAPTISTA.

Why, tell me, is not this my Cambio?

BIANCA.

Cambio is chang'd into Lucentio.

LUCENTIO.

Love wrought these miracles. Bianca's love

Made me exchange my state with Tranio,

While he did bear my countenance in the town;

And happily I have arriv'd at the last

Unto the wished haven of my bliss.

What Tranio did, myself enforc'd him to;

Then pardon him, sweet father, for my sake.

VINCENTIO.

I'll slit the villain's nose that would have sent me to the gaol.

BAPTISTA.

[To Lucentio.] But do you hear, sir? Have you married my daughter without asking my good will?

VINCENTIO.

Fear not, Baptista; we will content you, go to: but I will in, to be revenged for this villainy.

[Exit.]

BAPTISTA.

And I to sound the depth of this knavery.

[Exit.]

LUCENTIO.

Look not pale, Bianca; thy father will not frown.

[Exeunt Lucentio and Bianca.]

GREMIO.

My cake is dough, but I'll in among the rest;

Out of hope of all but my share of the feast.

[Exit.]

Petruchio and Katherina advance.

KATHERINA.

Husband, let's follow to see the end of this ado.

PETRUCHIO.

First kiss me, Kate, and we will.

KATHERINA.

What! in the midst of the street?

PETRUCHIO.

What! art thou ashamed of me?

KATHERINA.

No, sir; God forbid; but ashamed to kiss.

PETRUCHIO.

Why, then, let's home again. Come, sirrah, let's away.

KATHERINA.

Nay, I will give thee a kiss: now pray thee, love, stay.

PETRUCHIO.

Is not this well? Come, my sweet Kate:

Better once than never, for never too late.

[Exeunt.]

SCENE II. A room in LUCENTIO'S house.

Enter Baptista, Vincentio, Gremio, the Pedant, Lucentio, Bianca, Petruchio, Katherina, Hortensio and Widow. Tranio, Biondello and Grumio and Others, attending.

LUCENTIO.

At last, though long, our jarring notes agree:

And time it is when raging war is done,

To smile at 'scapes and perils overblown.

My fair Bianca, bid my father welcome,

While I with self-same kindness welcome thine.

Brother Petruchio, sister Katherina,

And thou, Hortensio, with thy loving widow,

Feast with the best, and welcome to my house:

My banquet is to close our stomachs up,

After our great good cheer. Pray you, sit down;

For now we sit to chat as well as eat.

[They sit at table.]

PETRUCHIO.

Nothing but sit and sit, and eat and eat!

BAPTISTA.

Padua affords this kindness, son Petruchio.

PETRUCHIO.

Padua affords nothing but what is kind.

HORTENSIO.

For both our sakes I would that word were true.

PETRUCHIO.

Now, for my life, Hortensio fears his widow.

WIDOW.

Then never trust me if I be afeard.

PETRUCHIO.

You are very sensible, and yet you miss my sense:

I mean Hortensio is afeard of you.

WIDOW.

He that is giddy thinks the world turns round.

PETRUCHIO.

Roundly replied.

KATHERINA.

Mistress, how mean you that?

WIDOW.

Thus I conceive by him.

PETRUCHIO.

Conceives by me! How likes Hortensio that?

HORTENSIO.

My widow says thus she conceives her tale.

PETRUCHIO.

Very well mended. Kiss him for that, good widow.

KATHERINA.

'He that is giddy thinks the world turns round':

I pray you tell me what you meant by that.

WIDOW.

Your husband, being troubled with a shrew,

Measures my husband's sorrow by his woe;

And now you know my meaning.

KATHERINA.

A very mean meaning.

WIDOW.

Right, I mean you.

KATHERINA.

And I am mean, indeed, respecting you.

PETRUCHIO.

To her, Kate!

HORTENSIO.

To her, widow!

PETRUCHIO.

A hundred marks, my Kate does put her down.

HORTENSIO.

That's my office.

PETRUCHIO.

Spoke like an officer: ha' to thee, lad.

[Drinks to Hortensio.]

BAPTISTA.

How likes Gremio these quick-witted folks?

GREMIO.

Believe me, sir, they butt together well.

BIANCA.

Head and butt! An hasty-witted body

Would say your head and butt were head and horn.

VINCENTIO.

Ay, mistress bride, hath that awaken'd you?

BIANCA.

Ay, but not frighted me; therefore I'll sleep again.

PETRUCHIO.

Nay, that you shall not; since you have begun,

Have at you for a bitter jest or two.

BIANCA.

Am I your bird? I mean to shift my bush,

And then pursue me as you draw your bow.

You are welcome all.

[Exeunt Bianca, Katherina and Widow.]

PETRUCHIO.

She hath prevented me. Here, Signior Tranio;

This bird you aim'd at, though you hit her not:

Therefore a health to all that shot and miss'd.

TRANIO.

O, sir! Lucentio slipp'd me like his greyhound,

Which runs himself, and catches for his master.

PETRUCHIO.

A good swift simile, but something currish.

TRANIO.

'Tis well, sir, that you hunted for yourself:

'Tis thought your deer does hold you at a bay.

BAPTISTA.

O ho, Petruchio! Tranio hits you now.

LUCENTIO.

I thank thee for that gird, good Tranio.

HORTENSIO.

Confess, confess; hath he not hit you here?

PETRUCHIO.

A has a little gall'd me, I confess;

And as the jest did glance away from me,

'Tis ten to one it maim'd you two outright.

BAPTISTA.

Now, in good sadness, son Petruchio,

I think thou hast the veriest shrew of all.

PETRUCHIO.

Well, I say no; and therefore, for assurance,

Let's each one send unto his wife,

And he whose wife is most obedient,

To come at first when he doth send for her,

Shall win the wager which we will propose.

HORTENSIO.

Content. What's the wager?

LUCENTIO.

Twenty crowns.

PETRUCHIO.

Twenty crowns!

I'll venture so much of my hawk or hound,

But twenty times so much upon my wife.

LUCENTIO.

A hundred then.

HORTENSIO.

Content.

PETRUCHIO.

A match! 'tis done.

HORTENSIO.

Who shall begin?

LUCENTIO.

That will I.

Go, Biondello, bid your mistress come to me.

BIONDELLO.

I go.

[Exit.]

BAPTISTA.

Son, I'll be your half, Bianca comes.

LUCENTIO.

I'll have no halves; I'll bear it all myself.

Re-enter Biondello.

How now! what news?

BIONDELLO.

Sir, my mistress sends you word

That she is busy and she cannot come.

PETRUCHIO.

How! She's busy, and she cannot come!

Is that an answer?

GREMIO.

Ay, and a kind one too:

Pray God, sir, your wife send you not a worse.

PETRUCHIO.

I hope better.

HORTENSIO.

Sirrah Biondello, go and entreat my wife

To come to me forthwith.

[Exit Biondello.]

PETRUCHIO.

O, ho! entreat her!

Nay, then she must needs come.

HORTENSIO.

I am afraid, sir,

Do what you can, yours will not be entreated.

Re-enter Biondello.

Now, where's my wife?

BIONDELLO.

She says you have some goodly jest in hand:

She will not come; she bids you come to her.

PETRUCHIO.

Worse and worse; she will not come! O vile,

Intolerable, not to be endur'd!

Sirrah Grumio, go to your mistress,

Say I command her come to me.

[Exit Grumio.]

HORTENSIO.

I know her answer.

PETRUCHIO.

What?

HORTENSIO.

She will not.

PETRUCHIO.

The fouler fortune mine, and there an end.

Re-enter Katherina.

BAPTISTA.

Now, by my holidame, here comes Katherina!

KATHERINA.

What is your will sir, that you send for me?

PETRUCHIO.

Where is your sister, and Hortensio's wife?

KATHERINA.

They sit conferring by the parlour fire.

PETRUCHIO.

Go fetch them hither; if they deny to come,

Swinge me them soundly forth unto their husbands.

Away, I say, and bring them hither straight.

[Exit Katherina.]

LUCENTIO.

Here is a wonder, if you talk of a wonder.

HORTENSIO.

And so it is. I wonder what it bodes.

PETRUCHIO.

Marry, peace it bodes, and love, and quiet life,

An awful rule, and right supremacy;

And, to be short, what not that's sweet and happy.

BAPTISTA.

Now fair befall thee, good Petruchio!

The wager thou hast won; and I will add

Unto their losses twenty thousand crowns;

Another dowry to another daughter,

For she is chang'd, as she had never been.

PETRUCHIO.

Nay, I will win my wager better yet,

And show more sign of her obedience,

Her new-built virtue and obedience.

See where she comes, and brings your froward wives

As prisoners to her womanly persuasion.

Re-enter Katherina with Bianca and Widow.

Katherine, that cap of yours becomes you not:

Off with that bauble, throw it underfoot.

[Katherina pulls off her cap and throws it down.]

WIDOW.

Lord, let me never have a cause to sigh

Till I be brought to such a silly pass!

BIANCA.

Fie! what a foolish duty call you this?

LUCENTIO.

I would your duty were as foolish too;

The wisdom of your duty, fair Bianca,

Hath cost me a hundred crowns since supper-time!

BIANCA.

The more fool you for laying on my duty.

PETRUCHIO.

Katherine, I charge thee, tell these headstrong women

What duty they do owe their lords and husbands.

WIDOW.

Come, come, you're mocking; we will have no telling.

PETRUCHIO.

Come on, I say; and first begin with her.

WIDOW.

She shall not.

PETRUCHIO.

I say she shall: and first begin with her.

KATHERINA.

Fie, fie! unknit that threatening unkind brow,

And dart not scornful glances from those eyes

To wound thy lord, thy king, thy governor:

It blots thy beauty as frosts do bite the meads,

Confounds thy fame as whirlwinds shake fair buds,

And in no sense is meet or amiable.

A woman mov'd is like a fountain troubled,

Muddy, ill-seeming, thick, bereft of beauty;

And while it is so, none so dry or thirsty

Will deign to sip or touch one drop of it.

Thy husband is thy lord, thy life, thy keeper,

Thy head, thy sovereign; one that cares for thee,

And for thy maintenance commits his body

To painful labour both by sea and land,

To watch the night in storms, the day in cold,

Whilst thou liest warm at home, secure and safe;

And craves no other tribute at thy hands

But love, fair looks, and true obedience;

Too little payment for so great a debt.

Such duty as the subject owes the prince,

Even such a woman oweth to her husband;

And when she is froward, peevish, sullen, sour,

And not obedient to his honest will,

What is she but a foul contending rebel

And graceless traitor to her loving lord?—

I am asham'd that women are so simple

To offer war where they should kneel for peace,

Or seek for rule, supremacy, and sway,

When they are bound to serve, love, and obey.

Why are our bodies soft and weak and smooth,

Unapt to toil and trouble in the world,

But that our soft conditions and our hearts

Should well agree with our external parts?

Come, come, you froward and unable worms!

My mind hath been as big as one of yours,

My heart as great, my reason haply more,

To bandy word for word and frown for frown;

But now I see our lances are but straws,

Our strength as weak, our weakness past compare,

That seeming to be most which we indeed least are.

Then vail your stomachs, for it is no boot,

And place your hands below your husband's foot:

In token of which duty, if he please,

My hand is ready; may it do him ease.

PETRUCHIO.

Why, there's a wench! Come on, and kiss me, Kate.

LUCENTIO.

Well, go thy ways, old lad, for thou shalt ha't.

VINCENTIO.

'Tis a good hearing when children are toward.

LUCENTIO.

But a harsh hearing when women are froward.

PETRUCHIO.

Come, Kate, we'll to bed.

We three are married, but you two are sped.

'Twas I won the wager,

[To Lucentio.] though you hit the white;

And being a winner, God give you good night!

[Exeunt Petrucio and Katherina.]

HORTENSIO.

Now go thy ways; thou hast tam'd a curst shrew.

LUCENTIO.

'Tis a wonder, by your leave, she will be tam'd so.

[Exeunt.]

ALL'S WELL THAT ENDS WELL

Dramatis Personæ

KING OF FRANCE.

THE DUKE OF FLORENCE.

BERTRAM, Count of Rossillon.

LAFEW, an old Lord.

PAROLLES, a follower of Bertram.

Several young French Lords, that serve with Bertram in the Florentine War.

RYNALDO, servant to the Countess of Rossillon.

Clown, servant to the Countess of Rossillon.

A Page, servant to the Countess of Rossillon.

COUNTESS OF ROSSILLON, mother to Bertram.

HELENA, a Gentlewoman protected by the Countess.

An old WIDOW of Florence.

DIANA, daughter to the Widow.

VIOLENTA, neighbour and friend to the Widow.

MARIANA, neighbour and friend to the Widow.

Lords attending on the KING; Officers; Soldiers, &c., French and Florentine.

SCENE: Partly in France, and partly in Tuscany.

ACT I

SCENE I. Rossillon. A room in the Countess's palace.

**Enter Bertram, the Countess of Rossillon, Helena, and Lafew, all in
black.**

COUNTESS.

In delivering my son from me, I bury a second husband.

BERTRAM.

And I in going, madam, weep o'er my father's death anew; but I must
attend his majesty's command, to whom I am now in ward, evermore in
subjection.

LAFEW.

You shall find of the king a husband, madam; you, sir, a father. He that
so generally is at all times good, must of necessity hold his virtue to you,
whose worthiness would stir it up where it wanted, rather than lack it where
there is such abundance.

COUNTESS.

What hope is there of his majesty's amendment?

LAFEW.

He hath abandon'd his physicians, madam; under whose practices he
hath persecuted time with hope, and finds no other advantage in the process
but only the losing of hope by time.

COUNTESS.

This young gentlewoman had a father—O that "had!", how sad a passage 'tis!—whose skill was almost as great as his honesty; had it stretch'd so far, would have made nature immortal, and death should have play for lack of work. Would for the king's sake he were living! I think it would be the death of the king's disease.

LAFEW.

How called you the man you speak of, madam?

COUNTESS.

He was famous, sir, in his profession, and it was his great right to be so: Gerard de Narbon.

LAFEW.

He was excellent indeed, madam; the king very lately spoke of him admiringly, and mourningly; he was skilful enough to have liv'd still, if knowledge could be set up against mortality.

BERTRAM.

What is it, my good lord, the king languishes of?

LAFEW.

A fistula, my lord.

BERTRAM.

I heard not of it before.

LAFEW.

I would it were not notorious. Was this gentlewoman the daughter of Gerard de Narbon?

COUNTESS.

His sole child, my lord, and bequeathed to my overlooking. I have those hopes of her good that her education promises her dispositions she inherits, which makes fair gifts fairer; for where an unclean mind carries virtuous qualities, there commendations go with pity, they are virtues and traitors too. In her they are the better for their simpleness; she derives her honesty, and achieves her goodness.

LAFEW.

Your commendations, madam, get from her tears.

COUNTESS.

'Tis the best brine a maiden can season her praise in. The remembrance of her father never approaches her heart but the tyranny of her sorrows takes all livelihood from her cheek. No more of this, Helena; go to, no more, lest it be rather thought you affect a sorrow than to have.

HELENA.

I do affect a sorrow indeed, but I have it too.

LAFEW.

Moderate lamentation is the right of the dead; excessive grief the enemy to the living.

COUNTESS.

If the living be enemy to the grief, the excess makes it soon mortal.

BERTRAM.

Madam, I desire your holy wishes.

LAFEW.

How understand we that?

COUNTESS.

Be thou blest, Bertram, and succeed thy father

In manners, as in shape! Thy blood and virtue

Contend for empire in thee, and thy goodness

Share with thy birthright! Love all, trust a few,

Do wrong to none. Be able for thine enemy

Rather in power than use; and keep thy friend

Under thy own life's key. Be check'd for silence,

But never tax'd for speech. What heaven more will,

That thee may furnish and my prayers pluck down,

Fall on thy head! Farewell. My lord,

'Tis an unseason'd courtier; good my lord,

Advise him.

LAFEW.

He cannot want the best

That shall attend his love.

COUNTESS.

Heaven bless him! Farewell, Bertram.

[Exit Countess.]

BERTRAM.

The best wishes that can be forg'd in your thoughts be servants to you! [To Helena.] Be comfortable to my mother, your mistress, and make much of her.

LAFEW.

Farewell, pretty lady, you must hold the credit of your father.

[Exeunt Bertram and Lafew.]

HELENA.

O, were that all! I think not on my father,

And these great tears grace his remembrance more

Than those I shed for him. What was he like?

I have forgot him; my imagination

Carries no favour in't but Bertram's.

I am undone: there is no living, none,

If Bertram be away. 'Twere all one

That I should love a bright particular star,

And think to wed it, he is so above me.

In his bright radiance and collateral light

Must I be comforted, not in his sphere.

Th'ambition in my love thus plagues itself:

The hind that would be mated by the lion

Must die for love. 'Twas pretty, though a plague,

To see him every hour; to sit and draw

His arched brows, his hawking eye, his curls,

In our heart's table,—heart too capable

Of every line and trick of his sweet favour.

But now he's gone, and my idolatrous fancy

Must sanctify his relics. Who comes here?

Enter Parolles.

One that goes with him: I love him for his sake,

And yet I know him a notorious liar,

Think him a great way fool, solely a coward;

Yet these fix'd evils sit so fit in him

That they take place when virtue's steely bones

Looks bleak i' th' cold wind: withal, full oft we see

Cold wisdom waiting on superfluous folly.

PAROLLES.

Save you, fair queen!

HELENA.

And you, monarch!

PAROLLES.

No.

HELENA.

And no.

PAROLLES.

Are you meditating on virginity?

HELENA.

Ay. You have some stain of soldier in you; let me ask you a question. Man is enemy to virginity; how may we barricado it against him?

PAROLLES.

Keep him out.

HELENA.

But he assails; and our virginity, though valiant, in the defence, yet is weak. Unfold to us some warlike resistance.

PAROLLES.

There is none. Man setting down before you will undermine you and blow you up.

HELENA.

Bless our poor virginity from underminers and blowers-up! Is there no military policy how virgins might blow up men?

PAROLLES.

Virginity being blown down, man will quicklier be blown up; marry, in blowing him down again, with the breach yourselves made, you lose your city. It is not politic in the commonwealth of nature to preserve virginity. Loss of virginity is rational increase, and there was never virgin got till virginity was first lost. That you were made of is metal to make virgins. Virginity, by being once lost, may be ten times found; by being ever kept, it is ever lost. 'Tis too cold a companion. Away with it!

HELENA.

I will stand for't a little, though therefore I die a virgin.

PAROLLES.

There's little can be said in't; 'tis against the rule of nature. To speak on the part of virginity is to accuse your mothers; which is most infallible disobedience. He that hangs himself is a virgin: virginity murders itself, and should be buried in highways out of all sanctified limit, as a desperate offendress against nature. Virginity breeds mites, much like a cheese; consumes itself to the very paring, and so dies with feeding his own stomach. Besides, virginity is peevish, proud, idle, made of self-love, which is the most inhibited sin in the canon. Keep it not; you cannot choose but lose by't. Out with't! Within the year it will make itself two, which is a goodly increase, and the principal itself not much the worse. Away with it!

HELENA.

How might one do, sir, to lose it to her own liking?

PAROLLES.

Let me see. Marry, ill, to like him that ne'er it likes. 'Tis a commodity will lose the gloss with lying; the longer kept, the less worth. Off with't while 'tis vendible; answer the time of request. Virginity, like an old courtier, wears her cap out of fashion, richly suited, but unsuitable, just like the brooch and the toothpick, which wear not now. Your date is better in your pie and your porridge than in your cheek. And your virginity, your old virginity, is like one of our French wither'd pears; it looks ill, it eats drily; marry, 'tis a wither'd pear; it was formerly better; marry, yet 'tis a wither'd pear. Will you anything with it?

HELENA.

Not my virginity yet.

There shall your master have a thousand loves,

A mother, and a mistress, and a friend,

A phoenix, captain, and an enemy,

A guide, a goddess, and a sovereign,

A counsellor, a traitress, and a dear:

His humble ambition, proud humility,

His jarring concord, and his discord dulcet,

His faith, his sweet disaster; with a world

Of pretty, fond, adoptious christendoms

That blinking Cupid gossips. Now shall he—

I know not what he shall. God send him well!

The court's a learning-place; and he is one.

PAROLLES.

What one, i' faith?

HELENA.

That I wish well. 'Tis pity—

PAROLLES.

What's pity?

HELENA.

That wishing well had not a body in't

Which might be felt, that we, the poorer born,

Whose baser stars do shut us up in wishes,

Might with effects of them follow our friends,

And show what we alone must think, which never

Returns us thanks.

Enter a Page.

PAGE.

Monsieur Parolles, my lord calls for you.

[Exit Page.]

PAROLLES.

Little Helen, farewell. If I can remember thee, I will think of thee at court.

HELENA.

Monsieur Parolles, you were born under a charitable star.

PAROLLES.

Under Mars, I.

HELENA.

I especially think, under Mars.

PAROLLES.

Why under Mars?

HELENA.

The wars hath so kept you under, that you must needs be born under Mars.

PAROLLES.

When he was predominant.

HELENA.

When he was retrograde, I think rather.

PAROLLES.

Why think you so?

HELENA.

You go so much backward when you fight.

PAROLLES.

That's for advantage.

HELENA.

So is running away, when fear proposes the safety: but the composition that your valour and fear makes in you is a virtue of a good wing, and I like the wear well.

PAROLLES.

I am so full of business I cannot answer thee acutely. I will return perfect courtier; in the which my instruction shall serve to naturalize thee, so thou wilt be capable of a courtier's counsel, and understand what advice shall thrust upon thee; else thou diest in thine unthankfulness, and thine ignorance makes thee away. Farewell. When thou hast leisure, say thy prayers; when thou hast none, remember thy friends. Get thee a good husband, and use him as he uses thee. So, farewell.

[Exit.]

HELENA.

Our remedies oft in ourselves do lie,

Which we ascribe to heaven: the fated sky

Gives us free scope; only doth backward pull

Our slow designs when we ourselves are dull.

What power is it which mounts my love so high,

That makes me see, and cannot feed mine eye?

The mightiest space in fortune nature brings

To join like likes, and kiss like native things.

Impossible be strange attempts to those

That weigh their pains in sense, and do suppose

What hath been cannot be. Who ever strove

To show her merit that did miss her love?

The king's disease,—my project may deceive me,

But my intents are fix'd, and will not leave me.

[Exit.]

183

SCENE II. Paris. A room in the King's palace.

Flourish of cornets. Enter the King of France, with letters; Lords and others attending.

KING.

The Florentines and Senoys are by th' ears;

Have fought with equal fortune, and continue

A braving war.

FIRST LORD.

So 'tis reported, sir.

KING.

Nay, 'tis most credible, we here receive it,

A certainty, vouch'd from our cousin Austria,

With caution, that the Florentine will move us

For speedy aid; wherein our dearest friend

Prejudicates the business, and would seem

To have us make denial.

FIRST LORD.

His love and wisdom,

Approv'd so to your majesty, may plead

For amplest credence.

KING.

He hath arm'd our answer,

And Florence is denied before he comes:

Yet, for our gentlemen that mean to see

The Tuscan service, freely have they leave

To stand on either part.

SECOND LORD.

It well may serve

A nursery to our gentry, who are sick

For breathing and exploit.

KING.

What's he comes here?

Enter Bertram, Lafew and Parolles.

FIRST LORD.

It is the Count Rossillon, my good lord,

Young Bertram.

KING.

Youth, thou bear'st thy father's face;

Frank nature, rather curious than in haste,

Hath well compos'd thee. Thy father's moral parts

Mayst thou inherit too! Welcome to Paris.

BERTRAM.

My thanks and duty are your majesty's.

KING.

I would I had that corporal soundness now,

As when thy father and myself in friendship

First tried our soldiership. He did look far

Into the service of the time, and was

Discipled of the bravest. He lasted long,

But on us both did haggish age steal on,

And wore us out of act. It much repairs me

To talk of your good father; in his youth

He had the wit which I can well observe

Today in our young lords; but they may jest

Till their own scorn return to them unnoted

Ere they can hide their levity in honour

So like a courtier, contempt nor bitterness

Were in his pride or sharpness; if they were,

His equal had awak'd them, and his honour,

Clock to itself, knew the true minute when

Exception bid him speak, and at this time

His tongue obey'd his hand. Who were below him

He us'd as creatures of another place,

And bow'd his eminent top to their low ranks,

Making them proud of his humility,

In their poor praise he humbled. Such a man

Might be a copy to these younger times;

Which, followed well, would demonstrate them now

But goers backward.

BERTRAM.

His good remembrance, sir,

Lies richer in your thoughts than on his tomb;

So in approof lives not his epitaph

As in your royal speech.

KING.

Would I were with him! He would always say,—

Methinks I hear him now; his plausive words

He scatter'd not in ears, but grafted them

To grow there and to bear,—"Let me not live,"

This his good melancholy oft began

On the catastrophe and heel of pastime,

When it was out,—"Let me not live" quoth he,

"After my flame lacks oil, to be the snuff

Of younger spirits, whose apprehensive senses

All but new things disdain; whose judgments are

Mere fathers of their garments; whose constancies

Expire before their fashions." This he wish'd.

I, after him, do after him wish too,

Since I nor wax nor honey can bring home,

I quickly were dissolved from my hive

To give some labourers room.

SECOND LORD.

You're lov'd, sir;

They that least lend it you shall lack you first.

KING.

I fill a place, I know't. How long is't, Count,

Since the physician at your father's died?

He was much fam'd.

BERTRAM.

Some six months since, my lord.

KING.

If he were living, I would try him yet;—

Lend me an arm;—the rest have worn me out

With several applications; nature and sickness

Debate it at their leisure. Welcome, Count;

My son's no dearer.

BERTRAM.

Thank your majesty.

[Exeunt. Flourish.]

SCENE III. Rossillon. A Room in the Palace.

Enter Countess, Steward and Clown.

COUNTESS.

I will now hear. What say you of this gentlewoman?

STEWARD.

Madam, the care I have had to even your content, I wish might be found in the calendar of my past endeavours; for then we wound our modesty, and make foul the clearness of our deservings, when of ourselves we publish them.

COUNTESS.

What does this knave here? Get you gone, sirrah. The complaints I have heard of you I do not all believe; 'tis my slowness that I do not; for I know you lack not folly to commit them, and have ability enough to make such knaveries yours.

CLOWN.

'Tis not unknown to you, madam, I am a poor fellow.

COUNTESS.

Well, sir.

CLOWN.

No, madam, 'tis not so well that I am poor, though many of the rich are damned; but if I may have your ladyship's good will to go to the world, Isbel the woman and I will do as we may.

COUNTESS.

Wilt thou needs be a beggar?

CLOWN.

I do beg your good will in this case.

COUNTESS.

In what case?

CLOWN.

In Isbel's case and mine own. Service is no heritage, and I think I shall never have the blessing of God till I have issue of my body; for they say barnes are blessings.

COUNTESS.

Tell me thy reason why thou wilt marry.

CLOWN.

My poor body, madam, requires it; I am driven on by the flesh, and he must needs go that the devil drives.

COUNTESS.

Is this all your worship's reason?

CLOWN.

Faith, madam, I have other holy reasons, such as they are.

COUNTESS.

May the world know them?

CLOWN.

I have been, madam, a wicked creature, as you and all flesh and blood are; and indeed I do marry that I may repent.

COUNTESS.

Thy marriage, sooner than thy wickedness.

CLOWN.

I am out of friends, madam, and I hope to have friends for my wife's sake.

COUNTESS.

Such friends are thine enemies, knave.

CLOWN.

Y'are shallow, madam, in great friends; for the knaves come to do that for me which I am a-weary of. He that ears my land spares my team, and gives me leave to in the crop: if I be his cuckold, he's my drudge. He that comforts my wife is the cherisher of my flesh and blood; he that cherishes my flesh and blood loves my flesh and blood; he that loves my flesh and blood is my friend; ergo, he that kisses my wife is my friend. If men could be contented to be what they are, there were no fear in marriage; for young Charbon the puritan and old Poysam the papist, howsome'er their hearts are sever'd in religion, their heads are both one; they may jowl horns together like any deer i' the herd.

COUNTESS.

Wilt thou ever be a foul-mouth'd and calumnious knave?

CLOWN.

A prophet I, madam; and I speak the truth the next way:

For I the ballad will repeat,

Which men full true shall find;

Your marriage comes by destiny,

Your cuckoo sings by kind.

COUNTESS.

Get you gone, sir; I'll talk with you more anon.

STEWARD.

May it please you, madam, that he bid Helen come to you; of her I am to speak.

COUNTESS.

Sirrah, tell my gentlewoman I would speak with her; Helen I mean.

CLOWN.

[Sings.]

Was this fair face the cause, quoth she,

Why the Grecians sacked Troy?

Fond done, done fond,

Was this King Priam's joy?

With that she sighed as she stood,

With that she sighed as she stood,

And gave this sentence then:

Among nine bad if one be good,

Among nine bad if one be good,

There's yet one good in ten.

COUNTESS.

What, one good in ten? You corrupt the song, sirrah.

CLOWN.

One good woman in ten, madam, which is a purifying o' the song. Would God would serve the world so all the year! We'd find no fault with the tithe-woman, if I were the parson. One in ten, quoth 'a! And we might have a good woman born but or every blazing star, or at an earthquake, 'twould mend the lottery well; a man may draw his heart out ere he pluck one.

COUNTESS.

You'll be gone, sir knave, and do as I command you!

CLOWN.

That man should be at woman's command, and yet no hurt done! Though honesty be no puritan, yet it will do no hurt; it will wear the surplice of humility over the black gown of a big heart. I am going, forsooth; the business is for Helen to come hither.

[Exit.]

COUNTESS.

Well, now.

STEWARD.

I know, madam, you love your gentlewoman entirely.

COUNTESS.

Faith I do. Her father bequeath'd her to me, and she herself, without other advantage, may lawfully make title to as much love as she finds; there is more owing her than is paid, and more shall be paid her than she'll demand.

STEWARD.

Madam, I was very late more near her than I think she wish'd me; alone she was, and did communicate to herself her own words to her own ears; she thought, I dare vow for her, they touch'd not any stranger sense. Her matter was, she loved your son. Fortune, she said, was no goddess, that had put such difference betwixt their two estates; Love no god, that would not extend his might only where qualities were level; Diana no queen of virgins, that would suffer her poor knight surpris'd, without rescue in the first assault or ransom afterward. This she deliver'd in the most bitter touch of sorrow that e'er I heard virgin exclaim in, which I held my duty speedily to acquaint you withal; sithence, in the loss that may happen, it concerns you something to know it.

COUNTESS.

You have discharg'd this honestly; keep it to yourself; many likelihoods inform'd me of this before, which hung so tottering in the balance that I could neither believe nor misdoubt. Pray you leave me; stall this in your bosom; and I thank you for your honest care. I will speak with you further anon.

[Exit Steward.]

Enter Helena.

Even so it was with me when I was young;

If ever we are nature's, these are ours; this thorn

Doth to our rose of youth rightly belong;

Our blood to us, this to our blood is born;

It is the show and seal of nature's truth,

Where love's strong passion is impress'd in youth.

By our remembrances of days foregone,

Such were our faults, or then we thought them none.

Her eye is sick on't; I observe her now.

HELENA.

What is your pleasure, madam?

COUNTESS.

You know, Helen,

I am a mother to you.

HELENA.

Mine honourable mistress.

COUNTESS.

Nay, a mother.

Why not a mother? When I said a mother,

Methought you saw a serpent. What's in mother,

That you start at it? I say I am your mother,

And put you in the catalogue of those

That were enwombed mine. 'Tis often seen

Adoption strives with nature, and choice breeds

A native slip to us from foreign seeds.

You ne'er oppress'd me with a mother's groan,

Yet I express to you a mother's care.

God's mercy, maiden! does it curd thy blood

To say I am thy mother? What's the matter,

That this distempered messenger of wet,

The many-colour'd Iris, rounds thine eye?

—Why, that you are my daughter?

HELENA.

That I am not.

COUNTESS.

I say, I am your mother.

HELENA.

Pardon, madam;

The Count Rossillon cannot be my brother.

I am from humble, he from honoured name;

No note upon my parents, his all noble,

My master, my dear lord he is; and I

His servant live, and will his vassal die.

He must not be my brother.

COUNTESS.

Nor I your mother?

HELENA.

You are my mother, madam; would you were—

So that my lord your son were not my brother,—

Indeed my mother! or were you both our mothers,

I care no more for than I do for heaven,

So I were not his sister. Can't no other,

But, I your daughter, he must be my brother?

COUNTESS.

Yes, Helen, you might be my daughter-in-law.

God shield you mean it not! daughter and mother

So strive upon your pulse. What! pale again?

My fear hath catch'd your fondness; now I see

The mystery of your loneliness, and find

Your salt tears' head. Now to all sense 'tis gross

You love my son; invention is asham'd,

Against the proclamation of thy passion

To say thou dost not. Therefore tell me true;

But tell me then, 'tis so; for, look, thy cheeks

Confess it, t'one to th'other; and thine eyes

See it so grossly shown in thy behaviours,

That in their kind they speak it; only sin

And hellish obstinacy tie thy tongue,

That truth should be suspected. Speak, is't so?

If it be so, you have wound a goodly clew;

If it be not, forswear't: howe'er, I charge thee,

As heaven shall work in me for thine avail,

To tell me truly.

HELENA.

Good madam, pardon me.

COUNTESS.

Do you love my son?

HELENA.

Your pardon, noble mistress.

COUNTESS.

Love you my son?

HELENA.

Do not you love him, madam?

COUNTESS.

Go not about; my love hath in't a bond

Whereof the world takes note. Come, come, disclose

The state of your affection, for your passions

Have to the full appeach'd.

HELENA.

Then I confess,

Here on my knee, before high heaven and you,

That before you, and next unto high heaven,

I love your son.

My friends were poor, but honest; so's my love.

Be not offended; for it hurts not him

That he is lov'd of me; I follow him not

By any token of presumptuous suit,

Nor would I have him till I do deserve him;

Yet never know how that desert should be.

I know I love in vain, strive against hope;

Yet in this captious and inteemable sieve

I still pour in the waters of my love

And lack not to lose still. Thus, Indian-like,

Religious in mine error, I adore

The sun that looks upon his worshipper,

But knows of him no more. My dearest madam,

Let not your hate encounter with my love,

For loving where you do; but if yourself,

Whose aged honour cites a virtuous youth,

Did ever, in so true a flame of liking,

Wish chastely, and love dearly, that your Dian

Was both herself and love; O then, give pity

To her whose state is such that cannot choose

But lend and give where she is sure to lose;

That seeks not to find that her search implies,

But riddle-like, lives sweetly where she dies!

COUNTESS.

Had you not lately an intent,—speak truly,—

To go to Paris?

HELENA.

Madam, I had.

COUNTESS.

Wherefore? tell true.

HELENA.

I will tell truth; by grace itself I swear.

You know my father left me some prescriptions

Of rare and prov'd effects, such as his reading

And manifest experience had collected

For general sovereignty; and that he will'd me

In heedfull'st reservation to bestow them,

As notes whose faculties inclusive were

More than they were in note. Amongst the rest

There is a remedy, approv'd, set down,

To cure the desperate languishings whereof

The king is render'd lost.

COUNTESS.

This was your motive

For Paris, was it? Speak.

HELENA.

My lord your son made me to think of this;

Else Paris, and the medicine, and the king,

Had from the conversation of my thoughts

Haply been absent then.

COUNTESS.

But think you, Helen,

If you should tender your supposed aid,

He would receive it? He and his physicians

Are of a mind; he, that they cannot help him;

They, that they cannot help. How shall they credit

A poor unlearned virgin, when the schools,

Embowell'd of their doctrine, have let off

The danger to itself?

HELENA.

There's something in't

More than my father's skill, which was the great'st

Of his profession, that his good receipt

Shall for my legacy be sanctified

By th' luckiest stars in heaven; and would your honour

But give me leave to try success, I'd venture

The well-lost life of mine on his grace's cure.

By such a day, an hour.

COUNTESS.

Dost thou believe't?

HELENA.

Ay, madam, knowingly.

COUNTESS.

Why, Helen, thou shalt have my leave and love,

Means and attendants, and my loving greetings

To those of mine in court. I'll stay at home,

And pray God's blessing into thy attempt.

Be gone tomorrow; and be sure of this,

What I can help thee to, thou shalt not miss.

[Exeunt.]

ACT II.

SCENE I. Paris. A room in the King's palace.

Flourish. Enter the King with young Lords taking leave for the Florentine war; Bertram, Parolles and Attendants.

KING.

Farewell, young lords; these warlike principles

Do not throw from you; and you, my lords, farewell;

Share the advice betwixt you; if both gain all,

The gift doth stretch itself as 'tis receiv'd,

And is enough for both.

FIRST LORD.

'Tis our hope, sir,

After well-ent'red soldiers, to return

And find your grace in health.

KING.

No, no, it cannot be; and yet my heart

Will not confess he owes the malady

That doth my life besiege. Farewell, young lords.

Whether I live or die, be you the sons

Of worthy Frenchmen; let higher Italy,—

Those bated that inherit but the fall

Of the last monarchy—see that you come

Not to woo honour, but to wed it, when

The bravest questant shrinks: find what you seek,

That fame may cry you loud. I say farewell.

SECOND LORD.

Health, at your bidding serve your majesty!

KING.

Those girls of Italy, take heed of them;

They say our French lack language to deny

If they demand; beware of being captives

Before you serve.

BOTH.

Our hearts receive your warnings.

KING.

Farewell.—Come hither to me.

[The King retires to a couch.]

FIRST LORD.

O my sweet lord, that you will stay behind us!

PAROLLES.

'Tis not his fault; the spark.

SECOND LORD.

O, 'tis brave wars!

PAROLLES.

Most admirable! I have seen those wars.

BERTRAM.

I am commanded here, and kept a coil with,

"Too young", and "the next year" and "'tis too early".

PAROLLES.

An thy mind stand to't, boy, steal away bravely.

BERTRAM.

I shall stay here the forehorse to a smock,

Creaking my shoes on the plain masonry,

Till honour be bought up, and no sword worn

But one to dance with. By heaven, I'll steal away.

FIRST LORD.

There's honour in the theft.

PAROLLES.

Commit it, count.

SECOND LORD.

I am your accessary; and so farewell.

BERTRAM.

I grow to you, and our parting is a tortur'd body.

FIRST LORD.

Farewell, captain.

SECOND LORD.

Sweet Monsieur Parolles!

PAROLLES.

Noble heroes, my sword and yours are kin. Good sparks and lustrous, a word, good metals. You shall find in the regiment of the Spinii one Captain Spurio, with his cicatrice, an emblem of war, here on his sinister cheek; it was this very sword entrench'd it. Say to him I live; and observe his reports for me.

FIRST LORD.

We shall, noble captain.

PAROLLES.

Mars dote on you for his novices!

[Exeunt Lords.]

What will ye do?

BERTRAM.

Stay the king.

PAROLLES.

Use a more spacious ceremony to the noble lords; you have restrain'd yourself within the list of too cold an adieu. Be more expressive to them; for they wear themselves in the cap of the time; there do muster true gait; eat, speak, and move, under the influence of the most receiv'd star; and though the devil lead the measure, such are to be followed. After them, and take a more dilated farewell.

BERTRAM.

And I will do so.

PAROLLES.

Worthy fellows, and like to prove most sinewy sword-men.

[Exeunt Bertram and Parolles.]

Enter Lafew.

LAFEW.

Pardon, my lord [kneeling], for me and for my tidings.

KING.

I'll fee thee to stand up.

LAFEW.

Then here's a man stands that has brought his pardon.

I would you had kneel'd, my lord, to ask me mercy,

And that at my bidding you could so stand up.

KING.

I would I had; so I had broke thy pate,

And ask'd thee mercy for't.

LAFEW.

Good faith, across;

But, my good lord, 'tis thus: will you be cur'd

Of your infirmity?

KING.

No.

LAFEW.

O, will you eat

No grapes, my royal fox? Yes, but you will

My noble grapes, and if my royal fox

Could reach them. I have seen a medicine

That's able to breathe life into a stone,

Quicken a rock, and make you dance canary

With sprightly fire and motion; whose simple touch

Is powerful to araise King Pippen, nay,

To give great Charlemain a pen in's hand

And write to her a love-line.

KING.

What 'her' is this?

LAFEW.

Why, doctor 'she'! My lord, there's one arriv'd,

If you will see her. Now, by my faith and honour,

If seriously I may convey my thoughts

In this my light deliverance, I have spoke

With one that in her sex, her years, profession,

Wisdom, and constancy, hath amaz'd me more

Than I dare blame my weakness. Will you see her,

For that is her demand, and know her business?

That done, laugh well at me.

KING.

Now, good Lafew,

Bring in the admiration; that we with thee

May spend our wonder too, or take off thine

By wond'ring how thou took'st it.

LAFEW.

Nay, I'll fit you,

And not be all day neither.

[Exit Lafew.]

KING.

Thus he his special nothing ever prologues.

Enter Lafew with Helena.

LAFEW.

Nay, come your ways.

KING.

This haste hath wings indeed.

LAFEW.

Nay, come your ways.

This is his majesty, say your mind to him.

A traitor you do look like, but such traitors

His majesty seldom fears; I am Cressid's uncle,

That dare leave two together. Fare you well.

[Exit.]

KING.

Now, fair one, does your business follow us?

HELENA.

Ay, my good lord.

Gerard de Narbon was my father,

In what he did profess, well found.

KING.

I knew him.

HELENA.

The rather will I spare my praises towards him.

Knowing him is enough. On his bed of death

Many receipts he gave me; chiefly one,

Which, as the dearest issue of his practice,

And of his old experience the only darling,

He bade me store up as a triple eye,

Safer than mine own two; more dear I have so,

And hearing your high majesty is touch'd

With that malignant cause, wherein the honour

Of my dear father's gift stands chief in power,

I come to tender it, and my appliance,

With all bound humbleness.

KING.

We thank you, maiden,

But may not be so credulous of cure,

When our most learned doctors leave us, and

The congregated college have concluded

That labouring art can never ransom nature

From her inaidable estate. I say we must not

So stain our judgment, or corrupt our hope,

To prostitute our past-cure malady

To empirics, or to dissever so

Our great self and our credit, to esteem

A senseless help, when help past sense we deem.

HELENA.

My duty then shall pay me for my pains.

I will no more enforce mine office on you,

Humbly entreating from your royal thoughts

A modest one to bear me back again.

KING.

I cannot give thee less, to be call'd grateful.

Thou thought'st to help me; and such thanks I give

As one near death to those that wish him live.

But what at full I know, thou know'st no part;

I knowing all my peril, thou no art.

HELENA.

What I can do can do no hurt to try,

Since you set up your rest 'gainst remedy.

He that of greatest works is finisher

Oft does them by the weakest minister.

So holy writ in babes hath judgment shown,

When judges have been babes. Great floods have flown

From simple sources, and great seas have dried

When miracles have by the great'st been denied.

Oft expectation fails, and most oft there

Where most it promises; and oft it hits

Where hope is coldest, and despair most fits.

KING.

I must not hear thee. Fare thee well, kind maid.

Thy pains, not us'd, must by thyself be paid;

Proffers, not took, reap thanks for their reward.

HELENA.

Inspired merit so by breath is barr'd.

It is not so with Him that all things knows

As 'tis with us that square our guess by shows;

But most it is presumption in us when

The help of heaven we count the act of men.

Dear sir, to my endeavours give consent;

Of heaven, not me, make an experiment.

I am not an impostor, that proclaim

Myself against the level of mine aim,

But know I think, and think I know most sure,

My art is not past power nor you past cure.

KING.

Art thou so confident? Within what space

Hop'st thou my cure?

HELENA.

The greatest grace lending grace.

Ere twice the horses of the sun shall bring

Their fiery torcher his diurnal ring,

Ere twice in murk and occidental damp

Moist Hesperus hath quench'd her sleepy lamp;

Or four and twenty times the pilot's glass

Hath told the thievish minutes how they pass;

What is infirm from your sound parts shall fly,

Health shall live free, and sickness freely die.

KING.

Upon thy certainty and confidence

What dar'st thou venture?

HELENA.

Tax of impudence,

A strumpet's boldness, a divulged shame,

Traduc'd by odious ballads; my maiden's name

Sear'd otherwise; ne worse of worst extended

With vildest torture, let my life be ended.

KING.

Methinks in thee some blessed spirit doth speak

His powerful sound within an organ weak;

And what impossibility would slay

In common sense, sense saves another way.

Thy life is dear, for all that life can rate

Worth name of life in thee hath estimate:

Youth, beauty, wisdom, courage, all

That happiness and prime can happy call.

Thou this to hazard needs must intimate

Skill infinite, or monstrous desperate.

Sweet practiser, thy physic I will try,

That ministers thine own death if I die.

HELENA.

If I break time, or flinch in property

Of what I spoke, unpitied let me die,

And well deserv'd. Not helping, death's my fee;

But if I help, what do you promise me?

KING.

Make thy demand.

HELENA.

But will you make it even?

KING.

Ay, by my sceptre and my hopes of heaven.

HELENA.

Then shalt thou give me, with thy kingly hand

What husband in thy power I will command:

Exempted be from me the arrogance

To choose from forth the royal blood of France,

My low and humble name to propagate

With any branch or image of thy state;

But such a one, thy vassal, whom I know

Is free for me to ask, thee to bestow.

KING.

Here is my hand; the premises observ'd,

Thy will by my performance shall be serv'd;

So make the choice of thy own time, for I,

Thy resolv'd patient, on thee still rely.

More should I question thee, and more I must,

Though more to know could not be more to trust:

From whence thou cam'st, how tended on; but rest

Unquestion'd welcome, and undoubted bless'd.

Give me some help here, ho! If thou proceed

As high as word, my deed shall match thy deed.

[Flourish. Exeunt.]

SCENE II. Rossillon. A room in the Countess's palace.

Enter Countess and Clown.

COUNTESS.

Come on, sir; I shall now put you to the height of your breeding.

CLOWN.

I will show myself highly fed and lowly taught. I know my business is but to the court.

COUNTESS.

To the court! Why, what place make you special, when you put off that with such contempt? But to the court!

CLOWN.

Truly, madam, if God have lent a man any manners, he may easily put it off at court: he that cannot make a leg, put off's cap, kiss his hand, and say nothing, has neither leg, hands, lip, nor cap; and indeed such a fellow, to say precisely, were not for the court; but for me, I have an answer will serve all men.

COUNTESS.

Marry, that's a bountiful answer that fits all questions.

CLOWN.

It is like a barber's chair, that fits all buttocks—the pin-buttock, the quatch-buttock, the brawn-buttock, or any buttock.

COUNTESS.

Will your answer serve fit to all questions?

CLOWN.

As fit as ten groats is for the hand of an attorney, as your French crown for your taffety punk, as Tib's rush for Tom's forefinger, as a pancake for Shrove-Tuesday, a morris for May-day, as the nail to his hole, the cuckold to his horn, as a scolding quean to a wrangling knave, as the nun's lip to the friar's mouth; nay, as the pudding to his skin.

COUNTESS.

Have you, I say, an answer of such fitness for all questions?

CLOWN.

From below your duke to beneath your constable, it will fit any question.

COUNTESS.

It must be an answer of most monstrous size that must fit all demands.

CLOWN.

But a trifle neither, in good faith, if the learned should speak truth of it. Here it is, and all that belongs to't. Ask me if I am a courtier; it shall do you no harm to learn.

COUNTESS.

To be young again, if we could: I will be a fool in question, hoping to be the wiser by your answer. I pray you, sir, are you a courtier?

CLOWN.

O Lord, sir! There's a simple putting off. More, more, a hundred of them.

COUNTESS.

Sir, I am a poor friend of yours, that loves you.

CLOWN.

O Lord, sir! Thick, thick; spare not me.

COUNTESS.

I think, sir, you can eat none of this homely meat.

CLOWN.

O Lord, sir! Nay, put me to't, I warrant you.

COUNTESS.

You were lately whipp'd, sir, as I think.

CLOWN.

O Lord, sir! Spare not me.

COUNTESS.

Do you cry 'O Lord, sir!' at your whipping, and 'spare not me'? Indeed your 'O Lord, sir!' is very sequent to your whipping. You would answer very well to a whipping, if you were but bound to't.

CLOWN.

I ne'er had worse luck in my life in my 'O Lord, sir!' I see things may serve long, but not serve ever.

COUNTESS.

I play the noble housewife with the time, to entertain it so merrily with a fool.

CLOWN.

O Lord, sir! Why, there't serves well again.

COUNTESS.

An end, sir! To your business. Give Helen this,

And urge her to a present answer back.

Commend me to my kinsmen and my son.

This is not much.

CLOWN.

Not much commendation to them?

COUNTESS.

Not much employment for you. You understand me?

CLOWN.

Most fruitfully. I am there before my legs.

COUNTESS.

Haste you again.

[Exeunt severally.]

SCENE III. Paris. The King's palace.

Enter Bertram, Lafew and Parolles.

LAFEW.

They say miracles are past; and we have our philosophical persons to make modern and familiar things supernatural and causeless. Hence is it that we make trifles of terrors, ensconcing ourselves into seeming knowledge when we should submit ourselves to an unknown fear.

PAROLLES.

Why, 'tis the rarest argument of wonder that hath shot out in our latter times.

BERTRAM.

And so 'tis.

LAFEW.

To be relinquish'd of the artists,—

PAROLLES.

So I say; both of Galen and Paracelsus.

LAFEW.

Of all the learned and authentic fellows,—

PAROLLES.

Right; so I say.

LAFEW.

That gave him out incurable,—

PAROLLES.

Why, there 'tis; so say I too.

LAFEW.

Not to be helped.

PAROLLES.

Right; as 'twere a man assur'd of a—

LAFEW.

Uncertain life and sure death.

PAROLLES.

Just; you say well. So would I have said.

LAFEW.

I may truly say, it is a novelty to the world.

PAROLLES.

It is indeed; if you will have it in showing, you shall read it in what do you call there?

LAFEW.

A showing of a heavenly effect in an earthly actor.

PAROLLES.

That's it; I would have said the very same.

LAFEW.

Why, your dolphin is not lustier; fore me, I speak in respect—

PAROLLES.

Nay, 'tis strange, 'tis very strange; that is the brief and the tedious of it; and he's of a most facinerious spirit that will not acknowledge it to be the—

LAFEW.

Very hand of heaven.

PAROLLES.

Ay, so I say.

LAFEW.

In a most weak—

PAROLLES.

And debile minister, great power, great transcendence, which should indeed give us a further use to be made than alone the recov'ry of the king, as to be—

LAFEW.

Generally thankful.

PAROLLES.

I would have said it; you say well. Here comes the king.

Enter King, Helena and Attendants.

LAFEW.

Lustique, as the Dutchman says. I'll like a maid the better, whilst I have a tooth in my head. Why, he's able to lead her a coranto.

PAROLLES.

Mor du vinager! is not this Helen?

LAFEW.

Fore God, I think so.

KING.

Go, call before me all the lords in court.

[Exit an Attendant.]

Sit, my preserver, by thy patient's side,

And with this healthful hand, whose banish'd sense

Thou has repeal'd, a second time receive

The confirmation of my promis'd gift,

Which but attends thy naming.

Enter several Lords.

Fair maid, send forth thine eye. This youthful parcel

Of noble bachelors stand at my bestowing,

O'er whom both sovereign power and father's voice

I have to use. Thy frank election make;

Thou hast power to choose, and they none to forsake.

HELENA.

To each of you one fair and virtuous mistress

Fall, when love please! Marry, to each but one!

LAFEW.

I'd give bay curtal and his furniture

My mouth no more were broken than these boys',

And writ as little beard.

KING.

Peruse them well.

Not one of those but had a noble father.

She addresses her to a Lord.

HELENA.

Gentlemen,

Heaven hath through me restor'd the king to health.

ALL.

We understand it, and thank heaven for you.

HELENA.

I am a simple maid, and therein wealthiest

That I protest I simply am a maid.

Please it, your majesty, I have done already.

The blushes in my cheeks thus whisper me:

"We blush that thou shouldst choose; but, be refused,

Let the white death sit on thy cheek for ever,

We'll ne'er come there again."

KING.

Make choice; and, see,

Who shuns thy love shuns all his love in me.

HELENA.

Now, Dian, from thy altar do I fly,

And to imperial Love, that god most high,

Do my sighs stream. [To first Lord.] Sir, will you hear my suit?

FIRST LORD.

And grant it.

HELENA.

Thanks, sir; all the rest is mute.

LAFEW.

I had rather be in this choice than throw ames-ace for my life.

HELENA.

[To second Lord.] The honour, sir, that flames in your fair eyes,

Before I speak, too threat'ningly replies.

Love make your fortunes twenty times above

Her that so wishes, and her humble love!

SECOND LORD.

No better, if you please.

HELENA.

My wish receive,

Which great Love grant; and so I take my leave.

LAFEW.

Do all they deny her? An they were sons of mine I'd have them whipp'd; or I would send them to th' Turk to make eunuchs of.

HELENA.

[To third Lord.] Be not afraid that I your hand should take;

I'll never do you wrong for your own sake.

Blessing upon your vows, and in your bed

Find fairer fortune, if you ever wed!

LAFEW.

These boys are boys of ice, they'll none have her. Sure, they are bastards to the English; the French ne'er got 'em.

HELENA.

[To fourth Lord.] You are too young, too happy, and too good,

To make yourself a son out of my blood.

FOURTH LORD.

Fair one, I think not so.

LAFEW.

There's one grape yet. I am sure thy father drank wine. But if thou beest not an ass, I am a youth of fourteen; I have known thee already.

HELENA.

[To Bertram.] I dare not say I take you, but I give

Me and my service, ever whilst I live,

Into your guiding power. This is the man.

KING.

Why, then, young Bertram, take her; she's thy wife.

BERTRAM.

My wife, my liege! I shall beseech your highness,

In such a business give me leave to use

The help of mine own eyes.

KING.

Know'st thou not, Bertram,

What she has done for me?

BERTRAM.

Yes, my good lord,

But never hope to know why I should marry her.

KING.

Thou know'st she has rais'd me from my sickly bed.

BERTRAM.

But follows it, my lord, to bring me down

Must answer for your raising? I know her well;

She had her breeding at my father's charge:

A poor physician's daughter my wife! Disdain

Rather corrupt me ever!

KING.

'Tis only title thou disdain'st in her, the which

I can build up. Strange is it that our bloods,

Of colour, weight, and heat, pour'd all together,

Would quite confound distinction, yet stands off

In differences so mighty. If she be

All that is virtuous, save what thou dislik'st,

A poor physician's daughter,—thou dislik'st—

Of virtue for the name. But do not so.

From lowest place when virtuous things proceed,

The place is dignified by the doer's deed.

Where great additions swell's, and virtue none,

It is a dropsied honour. Good alone

Is good without a name; vileness is so:

The property by what it is should go,

Not by the title. She is young, wise, fair;

In these to nature she's immediate heir;

And these breed honour: that is honour's scorn

Which challenges itself as honour's born,

And is not like the sire. Honours thrive

When rather from our acts we them derive

Than our fore-goers. The mere word's a slave,

Debauch'd on every tomb, on every grave

A lying trophy, and as oft is dumb

Where dust and damn'd oblivion is the tomb

Of honour'd bones indeed. What should be said?

If thou canst like this creature as a maid,

I can create the rest. Virtue and she

Is her own dower; honour and wealth from me.

BERTRAM.

I cannot love her, nor will strive to do 't.

KING.

Thou wrong'st thyself, if thou shouldst strive to choose.

HELENA.

That you are well restor'd, my lord, I am glad.

Let the rest go.

KING.

My honour's at the stake, which to defeat,

I must produce my power. Here, take her hand,

Proud scornful boy, unworthy this good gift,

That dost in vile misprision shackle up

My love and her desert; that canst not dream

We, poising us in her defective scale,

Shall weigh thee to the beam; that wilt not know

It is in us to plant thine honour where

We please to have it grow. Check thy contempt;

Obey our will, which travails in thy good;

Believe not thy disdain, but presently

Do thine own fortunes that obedient right

Which both thy duty owes and our power claims;

Or I will throw thee from my care for ever

Into the staggers and the careless lapse

Of youth and ignorance; both my revenge and hate

Loosing upon thee in the name of justice,

Without all terms of pity. Speak! Thine answer!

BERTRAM.

Pardon, my gracious lord; for I submit

My fancy to your eyes. When I consider

What great creation, and what dole of honour

Flies where you bid it, I find that she, which late

Was in my nobler thoughts most base, is now

The praised of the king; who, so ennobled,

Is as 'twere born so.

KING.

Take her by the hand,

And tell her she is thine; to whom I promise

A counterpoise; if not to thy estate,

A balance more replete.

BERTRAM.

I take her hand.

KING.

Good fortune and the favour of the king

Smile upon this contract; whose ceremony

Shall seem expedient on the now-born brief,

And be perform'd tonight. The solemn feast

Shall more attend upon the coming space,

Expecting absent friends. As thou lov'st her,

Thy love's to me religious; else, does err.

[Exeunt King, Bertram, Helena, Lords, and Attendants.]

LAFEW.

Do you hear, monsieur? A word with you.

PAROLLES.

Your pleasure, sir.

LAFEW.

Your lord and master did well to make his recantation.

PAROLLES.

Recantation! My lord! My master!

LAFEW.

Ay. Is it not a language I speak?

PAROLLES.

A most harsh one, and not to be understood without bloody succeeding. My master!

LAFEW.

Are you companion to the Count Rossillon?

PAROLLES.

To any count; to all counts; to what is man.

LAFEW.

To what is count's man: count's master is of another style.

PAROLLES.

You are too old, sir; let it satisfy you, you are too old.

LAFEW.

I must tell thee, sirrah, I write man; to which title age cannot bring thee.

PAROLLES.

What I dare too well do, I dare not do.

LAFEW.

I did think thee, for two ordinaries, to be a pretty wise fellow; thou didst make tolerable vent of thy travel; it might pass. Yet the scarfs and the bannerets about thee did manifoldly dissuade me from believing thee a vessel of too great a burden. I have now found thee; when I lose thee again I care not. Yet art thou good for nothing but taking up, and that thou art scarce worth.

PAROLLES.

Hadst thou not the privilege of antiquity upon thee—

LAFEW.

Do not plunge thyself too far in anger, lest thou hasten thy trial; which if—Lord have mercy on thee for a hen! So, my good window of lattice, fare thee well; thy casement I need not open, for I look through thee. Give me thy hand.

PAROLLES.

My lord, you give me most egregious indignity.

LAFEW.

Ay, with all my heart; and thou art worthy of it.

PAROLLES.

I have not, my lord, deserv'd it.

LAFEW.

Yes, good faith, every dram of it; and I will not bate thee a scruple.

PAROLLES.

Well, I shall be wiser.

LAFEW.

Ev'n as soon as thou canst, for thou hast to pull at a smack o' th' contrary. If ever thou beest bound in thy scarf and beaten, thou shalt find what it is to be proud of thy bondage. I have a desire to hold my acquaintance with thee, or rather my knowledge, that I may say in the default, "He is a man I know."

PAROLLES.

My lord, you do me most insupportable vexation.

LAFEW.

I would it were hell-pains for thy sake, and my poor doing eternal; for doing I am past, as I will by thee, in what motion age will give me leave.

[Exit.]

PAROLLES.

Well, thou hast a son shall take this disgrace off me; scurvy, old, filthy, scurvy lord! Well, I must be patient; there is no fettering of authority. I'll beat him, by my life, if I can meet him with any convenience, an he were double and double a lord. I'll have no more pity of his age than I would have of—I'll beat him, and if I could but meet him again.

Enter Lafew.

LAFEW.

Sirrah, your lord and master's married; there's news for you; you have a new mistress.

PAROLLES.

I most unfeignedly beseech your lordship to make some reservation of your wrongs. He is my good lord; whom I serve above is my master.

LAFEW.

Who? God?

PAROLLES.

Ay, sir.

LAFEW.

The devil it is that's thy master. Why dost thou garter up thy arms o' this fashion? Dost make hose of thy sleeves? Do other servants so? Thou wert best set thy lower part where thy nose stands. By mine honour, if I were but two hours younger, I'd beat thee. Methink'st thou art a general offence, and every man should beat thee. I think thou wast created for men to breathe themselves upon thee.

PAROLLES.

This is hard and undeserved measure, my lord.

LAFEW.

Go to, sir; you were beaten in Italy for picking a kernel out of a pomegranate; you are a vagabond, and no true traveller. You are more saucy with lords and honourable personages than the commission of your birth and virtue gives you heraldry. You are not worth another word, else I'd call you knave. I leave you.

[Exit.]

Enter Bertram.

PAROLLES.

Good, very good, it is so then. Good, very good; let it be conceal'd awhile.

BERTRAM.

Undone, and forfeited to cares for ever!

PAROLLES.

What's the matter, sweetheart?

BERTRAM.

Although before the solemn priest I have sworn,

I will not bed her.

PAROLLES.

What, what, sweetheart?

BERTRAM.

O my Parolles, they have married me!

I'll to the Tuscan wars, and never bed her.

PAROLLES.

France is a dog-hole, and it no more merits

The tread of a man's foot: to the wars!

BERTRAM.

There's letters from my mother; what th' import is

I know not yet.

PAROLLES.

Ay, that would be known. To th' wars, my boy, to th' wars!

He wears his honour in a box unseen

That hugs his kicky-wicky here at home,

Spending his manly marrow in her arms,

Which should sustain the bound and high curvet

Of Mars's fiery steed. To other regions!

France is a stable; we that dwell in't, jades,

Therefore, to th' war!

BERTRAM.

It shall be so; I'll send her to my house,

Acquaint my mother with my hate to her,

And wherefore I am fled; write to the king

That which I durst not speak. His present gift

Shall furnish me to those Italian fields

Where noble fellows strike. War is no strife

To the dark house and the detested wife.

PAROLLES.

Will this caprichio hold in thee, art sure?

BERTRAM.

Go with me to my chamber and advise me.

I'll send her straight away. Tomorrow

I'll to the wars, she to her single sorrow.

PAROLLES.

Why, these balls bound; there's noise in it. 'Tis hard:

A young man married is a man that's marr'd.

Therefore away, and leave her bravely; go.

The king has done you wrong; but hush 'tis so.

[Exeunt.]

SCENE IV. Paris. The King's palace.

Enter Helena and Clown.

HELENA.

My mother greets me kindly: is she well?

CLOWN.

She is not well, but yet she has her health; she's very merry, but yet she is not well. But thanks be given, she's very well, and wants nothing i' the world; but yet she is not well.

HELENA.

If she be very well, what does she ail that she's not very well?

CLOWN.

Truly, she's very well indeed, but for two things.

HELENA.

What two things?

CLOWN.

One, that she's not in heaven, whither God send her quickly! The other, that she's in earth, from whence God send her quickly!

Enter Parolles.

PAROLLES.

Bless you, my fortunate lady!

HELENA.

I hope, sir, I have your good will to have mine own good fortune.

PAROLLES.

You had my prayers to lead them on; and to keep them on, have them still. O, my knave how does my old lady?

CLOWN.

So that you had her wrinkles and I her money, I would she did as you say.

PAROLLES.

Why, I say nothing.

CLOWN.

Marry, you are the wiser man; for many a man's tongue shakes out his master's undoing. To say nothing, to do nothing, to know nothing, and to have nothing, is to be a great part of your title; which is within a very little of nothing.

PAROLLES.

Away! Thou art a knave.

CLOWN.

You should have said, sir, before a knave thou art a knave; that is before me thou art a knave. This had been truth, sir.

PAROLLES.

Go to, thou art a witty fool; I have found thee.

CLOWN.

Did you find me in yourself, sir? or were you taught to find me? The search, sir, was profitable; and much fool may you find in you, even to the world's pleasure and the increase of laughter.

PAROLLES.

A good knave, i' faith, and well fed.

Madam, my lord will go away tonight;

A very serious business calls on him.

The great prerogative and right of love,

Which, as your due, time claims, he does acknowledge;

But puts it off to a compell'd restraint;

Whose want, and whose delay, is strew'd with sweets;

Which they distil now in the curbed time,

To make the coming hour o'erflow with joy

And pleasure drown the brim.

HELENA.

What's his will else?

PAROLLES.

That you will take your instant leave o' the king,

And make this haste as your own good proceeding,

Strengthen'd with what apology you think

May make it probable need.

HELENA.

What more commands he?

PAROLLES.

That, having this obtain'd, you presently

Attend his further pleasure.

HELENA.

In everything I wait upon his will.

PAROLLES.

I shall report it so.

HELENA.

I pray you. Come, sirrah.

[Exeunt.]

SCENE V. Another room in the same.

Enter Lafew and Bertram.

LAFEW.

But I hope your lordship thinks not him a soldier.

BERTRAM.

Yes, my lord, and of very valiant approof.

LAFEW.

You have it from his own deliverance.

BERTRAM.

And by other warranted testimony.

LAFEW.

Then my dial goes not true; I took this lark for a bunting.

BERTRAM.

I do assure you, my lord, he is very great in knowledge, and accordingly valiant.

LAFEW.

I have, then, sinned against his experience and transgressed against his valour; and my state that way is dangerous, since I cannot yet find in my heart to repent. Here he comes; I pray you make us friends; I will pursue the amity

Enter Parolles.

PAROLLES.

[To Bertram.] These things shall be done, sir.

LAFEW.

Pray you, sir, who's his tailor?

PAROLLES.

Sir!

LAFEW.

O, I know him well, I, sir; he, sir, is a good workman, a very good tailor.

BERTRAM.

[Aside to Parolles.] Is she gone to the king?

PAROLLES.

She is.

BERTRAM.

Will she away tonight?

PAROLLES.

As you'll have her.

BERTRAM.

I have writ my letters, casketed my treasure,

Given order for our horses; and tonight,

When I should take possession of the bride,

End ere I do begin.

LAFEW.

A good traveller is something at the latter end of a dinner; but one that lies three-thirds and uses a known truth to pass a thousand nothings with, should be once heard and thrice beaten.— God save you, Captain.

BERTRAM.

Is there any unkindness between my lord and you, monsieur?

PAROLLES.

I know not how I have deserved to run into my lord's displeasure.

LAFEW.

You have made shift to run into 't, boots and spurs and all, like him that leapt into the custard; and out of it you'll run again, rather than suffer question for your residence.

BERTRAM.

It may be you have mistaken him, my lord.

LAFEW.

And shall do so ever, though I took him at his prayers. Fare you well, my lord; and believe this of me, there can be no kernal in this light nut; the soul of this man is his clothes; trust him not in matter of heavy consequence; I have kept of them tame, and know their natures. Farewell, monsieur; I have spoken better of you than you have or will to deserve at my hand; but we must do good against evil.

[Exit.]

PAROLLES.

An idle lord, I swear.

BERTRAM.

I think so.

PAROLLES.

Why, do you not know him?

BERTRAM.

Yes, I do know him well; and common speech

Gives him a worthy pass. Here comes my clog.

Enter Helena.

HELENA.

I have, sir, as I was commanded from you,

Spoke with the king, and have procur'd his leave

For present parting; only he desires

Some private speech with you.

BERTRAM.

I shall obey his will.

You must not marvel, Helen, at my course,

Which holds not colour with the time, nor does

The ministration and required office

On my particular. Prepared I was not

For such a business; therefore am I found

So much unsettled: this drives me to entreat you;

That presently you take your way for home,

And rather muse than ask why I entreat you:

For my respects are better than they seem;

And my appointments have in them a need

Greater than shows itself at the first view

To you that know them not. This to my mother.

[Giving a letter.]

'Twill be two days ere I shall see you; so

I leave you to your wisdom.

HELENA.

Sir, I can nothing say

But that I am your most obedient servant.

BERTRAM.

Come, come, no more of that.

HELENA.

And ever shall

With true observance seek to eke out that

Wherein toward me my homely stars have fail'd

To equal my great fortune.

BERTRAM.

Let that go.

My haste is very great. Farewell; hie home.

HELENA.

Pray, sir, your pardon.

BERTRAM.

Well, what would you say?

HELENA.

I am not worthy of the wealth I owe;

Nor dare I say 'tis mine, and yet it is;

But, like a timorous thief, most fain would steal

What law does vouch mine own.

BERTRAM.

What would you have?

HELENA.

Something; and scarce so much; nothing indeed.

I would not tell you what I would, my lord. Faith, yes,

Strangers and foes do sunder and not kiss.

BERTRAM.

I pray you, stay not, but in haste to horse.

HELENA.

I shall not break your bidding, good my lord.

Where are my other men, monsieur?

Farewell,

[Exit Helena.]

BERTRAM.

Go thou toward home, where I will never come

Whilst I can shake my sword or hear the drum.

Away, and for our flight.

PAROLLES.

Bravely, coragio!

[Exeunt.]

ACT III.

SCENE I. Florence. A room in the Duke's palace.

Flourish. Enter the Duke of Florence attended; two French Lords, and Soldiers.

DUKE.

So that, from point to point, now have you heard

The fundamental reasons of this war,

Whose great decision hath much blood let forth,

And more thirsts after.

FIRST LORD.

Holy seems the quarrel

Upon your Grace's part; black and fearful

On the opposer.

DUKE.

Therefore we marvel much our cousin France

Would, in so just a business, shut his bosom

Against our borrowing prayers.

SECOND LORD.

Good my lord,

The reasons of our state I cannot yield,

But like a common and an outward man

That the great figure of a council frames

By self-unable motion; therefore dare not

Say what I think of it, since I have found

Myself in my incertain grounds to fail

As often as I guess'd.

DUKE.

Be it his pleasure.

FIRST LORD.

But I am sure the younger of our nature,

That surfeit on their ease, will day by day

Come here for physic.

DUKE.

Welcome shall they be;

And all the honours that can fly from us

Shall on them settle. You know your places well;

When better fall, for your avails they fell.

Tomorrow to the field.

[Flourish. Exeunt.]

SCENE II. Rossillon. A room in the Countess's palace.

Enter Countess and Clown.

COUNTESS.

It hath happen'd all as I would have had it, save that he comes not along with her.

CLOWN.

By my troth, I take my young lord to be a very melancholy man.

COUNTESS.

By what observance, I pray you?

CLOWN.

Why, he will look upon his boot and sing; mend the ruff and sing; ask questions and sing; pick his teeth and sing. I know a man that had this trick of melancholy sold a goodly manor for a song.

COUNTESS.

Let me see what he writes, and when he means to come.

[Opening a letter.]

CLOWN.

I have no mind to Isbel since I was at court. Our old lings and our Isbels o' th' country are nothing like your old ling and your Isbels o' th' court. The brains of my Cupid's knock'd out, and I begin to love, as an old man loves money, with no stomach.

COUNTESS.

What have we here?

CLOWN.

E'en that you have there.

[Exit.]

COUNTESS.

[Reads.] I have sent you a daughter-in-law; she hath recovered the king and undone me. I have wedded her, not bedded her, and sworn to make the "not" eternal. You shall hear I am run away; know it before the report come. If there be breadth enough in the world, I will hold a long distance. My duty to you.

Your unfortunate son,

BERTRAM.

This is not well, rash and unbridled boy,

To fly the favours of so good a king,

To pluck his indignation on thy head

By the misprizing of a maid too virtuous

For the contempt of empire.

Enter Clown.

CLOWN.

O madam, yonder is heavy news within between two soldiers and my young lady.

COUNTESS.

What is the matter?

CLOWN.

Nay, there is some comfort in the news, some comfort; your son will not be kill'd so soon as I thought he would.

COUNTESS.

Why should he be kill'd?

CLOWN.

So say I, madam, if he run away, as I hear he does; the danger is in standing to't; that's the loss of men, though it be the getting of children. Here they come will tell you more. For my part, I only hear your son was run away.

[Exit.]

Enter Helena and the two Gentlemen.

FIRST GENTLEMAN.

Save you, good madam.

HELENA.

Madam, my lord is gone, for ever gone.

SECOND GENTLEMAN.

Do not say so.

COUNTESS.

Think upon patience. Pray you, gentlemen,—

I have felt so many quirks of joy and grief

That the first face of neither on the start

Can woman me unto 't. Where is my son, I pray you?

SECOND GENTLEMAN.

Madam, he's gone to serve the Duke of Florence;

We met him thitherward, for thence we came,

And, after some despatch in hand at court,

Thither we bend again.

HELENA.

Look on this letter, madam; here's my passport.

[Reads.] When thou canst get the ring upon my finger, which never shall come off, and show me a child begotten of thy body that I am father to, then call me husband; but in such a "then" I write a "never".

This is a dreadful sentence.

COUNTESS.

Brought you this letter, gentlemen?

FIRST GENTLEMAN.

Ay, madam; And for the contents' sake, are sorry for our pains.

COUNTESS.

I pr'ythee, lady, have a better cheer;

If thou engrossest all the griefs are thine,

Thou robb'st me of a moiety. He was my son,

But I do wash his name out of my blood,

And thou art all my child. Towards Florence is he?

SECOND GENTLEMAN.

Ay, madam.

COUNTESS.

And to be a soldier?

SECOND GENTLEMAN.

Such is his noble purpose, and, believe't,

The duke will lay upon him all the honour

That good convenience claims.

COUNTESS.

Return you thither?

FIRST GENTLEMAN.

Ay, madam, with the swiftest wing of speed.

HELENA.

[Reads.] Till I have no wife, I have nothing in France.

'Tis bitter.

COUNTESS.

Find you that there?

HELENA.

Ay, madam.

FIRST GENTLEMAN.

'Tis but the boldness of his hand haply, which his heart was not consenting to.

COUNTESS.

Nothing in France until he have no wife!

There's nothing here that is too good for him

But only she, and she deserves a lord

That twenty such rude boys might tend upon,

And call her hourly mistress. Who was with him?

FIRST GENTLEMAN.

A servant only, and a gentleman which I have sometime known.

COUNTESS.

Parolles, was it not?

FIRST GENTLEMAN.

252

Ay, my good lady, he.

COUNTESS.

A very tainted fellow, and full of wickedness.

My son corrupts a well-derived nature

With his inducement.

FIRST GENTLEMAN.

Indeed, good lady,

The fellow has a deal of that too much,

Which holds him much to have.

COUNTESS.

Y'are welcome, gentlemen.

I will entreat you, when you see my son,

To tell him that his sword can never win

The honour that he loses: more I'll entreat you

Written to bear along.

SECOND GENTLEMAN.

We serve you, madam,

In that and all your worthiest affairs.

COUNTESS.

Not so, but as we change our courtesies.

Will you draw near?

[Exeunt Countess and Gentlemen.]

HELENA.

"Till I have no wife, I have nothing in France."

Nothing in France until he has no wife!

Thou shalt have none, Rossillon, none in France;

Then hast thou all again. Poor lord, is't I

That chase thee from thy country, and expose

Those tender limbs of thine to the event

Of the none-sparing war? And is it I

That drive thee from the sportive court, where thou

Wast shot at with fair eyes, to be the mark

Of smoky muskets? O you leaden messengers,

That ride upon the violent speed of fire,

Fly with false aim; move the still-peering air,

That sings with piercing; do not touch my lord.

Whoever shoots at him, I set him there;

Whoever charges on his forward breast,

I am the caitiff that do hold him to't;

And though I kill him not, I am the cause

His death was so effected. Better 'twere

I met the ravin lion when he roar'd

With sharp constraint of hunger; better 'twere

That all the miseries which nature owes

Were mine at once. No; come thou home, Rossillon,

Whence honour but of danger wins a scar,

As oft it loses all. I will be gone;

My being here it is that holds thee hence.

Shall I stay here to do't? No, no, although

The air of paradise did fan the house,

And angels offic'd all. I will be gone,

That pitiful rumour may report my flight

To consolate thine ear. Come, night; end, day;

For with the dark, poor thief, I'll steal away.

[Exit.]

255

SCENE III. Florence. Before the Duke's palace.

Flourish. Enter the Duke of Florence, Bertram, drum and trumpets, Soldiers, Parolles.

DUKE.

The general of our horse thou art, and we,

Great in our hope, lay our best love and credence

Upon thy promising fortune.

BERTRAM.

Sir, it is

A charge too heavy for my strength; but yet

We'll strive to bear it for your worthy sake

To th'extreme edge of hazard.

DUKE.

Then go thou forth;

And fortune play upon thy prosperous helm,

As thy auspicious mistress!

BERTRAM.

This very day,

Great Mars, I put myself into thy file;

Make me but like my thoughts, and I shall prove

A lover of thy drum, hater of love.

[Exeunt.]

SCENE IV. Rossillon. A room in the Countess's palace.

Enter Countess and Steward.

COUNTESS.

Alas! and would you take the letter of her?

Might you not know she would do as she has done,

By sending me a letter? Read it again.

STEWARD.

[Reads.] I am Saint Jaques' pilgrim, thither gone.

Ambitious love hath so in me offended

That barefoot plod I the cold ground upon,

With sainted vow my faults to have amended.

Write, write, that from the bloody course of war

My dearest master, your dear son, may hie.

Bless him at home in peace, whilst I from far

His name with zealous fervour sanctify.

His taken labours bid him me forgive;

I, his despiteful Juno, sent him forth

From courtly friends, with camping foes to live,

Where death and danger dog the heels of worth.

He is too good and fair for death and me;

Whom I myself embrace to set him free.

COUNTESS.

Ah, what sharp stings are in her mildest words!

Rynaldo, you did never lack advice so much

As letting her pass so; had I spoke with her,

I could have well diverted her intents,

Which thus she hath prevented.

STEWARD.

Pardon me, madam;

If I had given you this at over-night,

She might have been o'erta'en; and yet she writes

Pursuit would be but vain.

COUNTESS.

What angel shall

Bless this unworthy husband? He cannot thrive,

Unless her prayers, whom heaven delights to hear

And loves to grant, reprieve him from the wrath

Of greatest justice. Write, write, Rynaldo,

To this unworthy husband of his wife;

Let every word weigh heavy of her worth,

That he does weigh too light; my greatest grief,

Though little he do feel it, set down sharply.

Dispatch the most convenient messenger.

When haply he shall hear that she is gone

He will return; and hope I may that she,

Hearing so much, will speed her foot again,

Led hither by pure love. Which of them both

Is dearest to me I have no skill in sense

To make distinction. Provide this messenger.

My heart is heavy, and mine age is weak;

Grief would have tears, and sorrow bids me speak.

[Exeunt.]

SCENE V. Without the walls of Florence.

Enter an old Widow of Florence, Diana, Violenta, Mariana and other Citizens.

WIDOW.

Nay, come; for if they do approach the city, we shall lose all the sight.

DIANA.

They say the French count has done most honourable service.

WIDOW.

It is reported that he has taken their great'st commander, and that with his own hand he slew the duke's brother.

[A tucket afar off.]

We have lost our labour; they are gone a contrary way. Hark! you may know by their trumpets.

MARIANA.

Come, let's return again, and suffice ourselves with the report of it. Well, Diana, take heed of this French earl; the honour of a maid is her name; and no legacy is so rich as honesty.

WIDOW.

I have told my neighbour how you have been solicited by a gentleman his companion.

MARIANA.

I know that knave; hang him! one Parolles; a filthy officer he is in those suggestions for the young earl. Beware of them, Diana; their promises, enticements, oaths, tokens, and all these engines of lust, are not the things they go under; many a maid hath been seduced by them; and the misery is, example, that so terrible shows in the wreck of maidenhood, cannot for all that dissuade succession, but that they are limed with the twigs that threaten them. I hope I need not to advise you further; but I hope your own grace will keep you where you are, though there were no further danger known but the modesty which is so lost.

DIANA.

You shall not need to fear me.

Enter Helena in the dress of a pilgrim.

WIDOW.

I hope so. Look, here comes a pilgrim. I know she will lie at my house; thither they send one another; I'll question her. God save you, pilgrim! Whither are bound?

HELENA.

To Saint Jaques le Grand.

Where do the palmers lodge, I do beseech you?

WIDOW.

At the Saint Francis here, beside the port.

HELENA.

Is this the way?

[A march afar.]

WIDOW.

Ay, marry, is't. Hark you, they come this way.

If you will tarry, holy pilgrim,

But till the troops come by,

I will conduct you where you shall be lodg'd;

The rather for I think I know your hostess

As ample as myself.

HELENA.

Is it yourself?

WIDOW.

If you shall please so, pilgrim.

HELENA.

I thank you, and will stay upon your leisure.

WIDOW.

You came, I think, from France?

HELENA.

I did so.

WIDOW.

Here you shall see a countryman of yours

That has done worthy service.

HELENA.

His name, I pray you.

DIANA.

The Count Rossillon. Know you such a one?

HELENA.

But by the ear, that hears most nobly of him;

His face I know not.

DIANA.

Whatsome'er he is,

He's bravely taken here. He stole from France,

As 'tis reported, for the king had married him

Against his liking. Think you it is so?

HELENA.

Ay, surely, mere the truth; I know his lady.

DIANA.

There is a gentleman that serves the count

Reports but coarsely of her.

HELENA.

What's his name?

DIANA.

Monsieur Parolles.

HELENA.

O, I believe with him,

In argument of praise, or to the worth

Of the great count himself, she is too mean

To have her name repeated; all her deserving

Is a reserved honesty, and that

I have not heard examin'd.

DIANA.

Alas, poor lady!

'Tis a hard bondage to become the wife

Of a detesting lord.

WIDOW.

Ay, right; good creature, wheresoe'er she is,

Her heart weighs sadly. This young maid might do her

A shrewd turn, if she pleas'd.

HELENA.

How do you mean?

Maybe the amorous count solicits her

In the unlawful purpose.

WIDOW.

He does indeed,

And brokes with all that can in such a suit

Corrupt the tender honour of a maid;

But she is arm'd for him, and keeps her guard

In honestest defence.

Enter, with a drum and colours, a party of the Florentine army, Bertram and Parolles.

MARIANA.

The gods forbid else!

WIDOW.

So, now they come.

That is Antonio, the Duke's eldest son;

That Escalus.

HELENA.

Which is the Frenchman?

DIANA.

He;

That with the plume; 'tis a most gallant fellow.

I would he lov'd his wife; if he were honester

He were much goodlier. Is't not a handsome gentleman?

HELENA.

I like him well.

DIANA.

'Tis pity he is not honest. Yond's that same knave

That leads him to these places. Were I his lady

I would poison that vile rascal.

HELENA.

Which is he?

DIANA.

That jack-an-apes with scarfs. Why is he melancholy?

HELENA.

Perchance he's hurt i' the battle.

PAROLLES.

Lose our drum! Well.

MARIANA.

He's shrewdly vex'd at something. Look, he has spied us.

WIDOW.

Marry, hang you!

MARIANA.

And your courtesy, for a ring-carrier!

[Exeunt Bertram, Parolles, Officers and Soldiers.]

WIDOW.

The troop is past. Come, pilgrim, I will bring you

Where you shall host; of enjoin'd penitents

There's four or five, to great Saint Jaques bound,

Already at my house.

HELENA.

I humbly thank you.

Please it this matron and this gentle maid

To eat with us tonight; the charge and thanking

Shall be for me; and, to requite you further,

I will bestow some precepts of this virgin,

Worthy the note.

BOTH.

We'll take your offer kindly.

[Exeunt.]

SCENE VI. Camp before Florence.

Enter Bertram and the two French Lords.

FIRST LORD.

Nay, good my lord, put him to't; let him have his way.

SECOND LORD.

If your lordship find him not a hilding, hold me no more in your respect.

FIRST LORD.

On my life, my lord, a bubble.

BERTRAM.

Do you think I am so far deceived in him?

FIRST LORD.

Believe it, my lord, in mine own direct knowledge, without any malice, but to speak of him as my kinsman, he's a most notable coward, an infinite and endless liar, an hourly promise-breaker, the owner of no one good quality worthy your lordship's entertainment.

SECOND LORD.

It were fit you knew him; lest, reposing too far in his virtue, which he hath not, he might at some great and trusty business, in a main danger fail you.

BERTRAM.

I would I knew in what particular action to try him.

SECOND LORD.

None better than to let him fetch off his drum, which you hear him so confidently undertake to do.

FIRST LORD.

I with a troop of Florentines will suddenly surprise him; such I will have whom I am sure he knows not from the enemy; we will bind and hoodwink him so that he shall suppose no other but that he is carried into the leaguer of the adversaries when we bring him to our own tents. Be but your lordship present at his examination; if he do not for the promise of his life, and in the highest compulsion of base fear, offer to betray you, and deliver all the intelligence in his power against you, and that with the divine forfeit of his soul upon oath, never trust my judgment in anything.

SECOND LORD.

O, for the love of laughter, let him fetch his drum; he says he has a stratagem for't. When your lordship sees the bottom of his success in't, and to what metal this counterfeit lump of ore will be melted, if you give him not John Drum's entertainment, your inclining cannot be removed. Here he comes.

Enter Parolles.

FIRST LORD.

O, for the love of laughter, hinder not the honour of his design: let him fetch off his drum in any hand.

BERTRAM.

How now, monsieur! This drum sticks sorely in your disposition.

SECOND LORD.

A pox on 't; let it go; 'tis but a drum.

PAROLLES.

But a drum! Is't but a drum? A drum so lost! There was excellent command, to charge in with our horse upon our own wings, and to rend our own soldiers.

SECOND LORD.

That was not to be blam'd in the command of the service; it was a disaster of war that Caesar himself could not have prevented, if he had been there to command.

BERTRAM.

Well, we cannot greatly condemn our success: some dishonour we had in the loss of that drum, but it is not to be recovered.

PAROLLES.

It might have been recovered.

BERTRAM.

It might, but it is not now.

PAROLLES.

It is to be recovered. But that the merit of service is seldom attributed to the true and exact performer, I would have that drum or another, or hic jacet.

BERTRAM.

Why, if you have a stomach, to't, monsieur, if you think your mystery in stratagem can bring this instrument of honour again into his native quarter, be magnanimous in the enterprise, and go on; I will grace the attempt for a worthy exploit; if you speed well in it, the duke shall both speak of it and extend to you what further becomes his greatness, even to the utmost syllable of your worthiness.

PAROLLES.

By the hand of a soldier, I will undertake it.

BERTRAM.

But you must not now slumber in it.

PAROLLES.

I'll about it this evening; and I will presently pen down my dilemmas, encourage myself in my certainty, put myself into my mortal preparation; and by midnight look to hear further from me.

BERTRAM.

May I be bold to acquaint his grace you are gone about it?

PAROLLES.

I know not what the success will be, my lord, but the attempt I vow.

BERTRAM.

I know th'art valiant; and to the possibility of thy soldiership, will subscribe for thee. Farewell.

PAROLLES.

I love not many words.

[Exit.]

FIRST LORD.

No more than a fish loves water. Is not this a strange fellow, my lord, that so confidently seems to undertake this business, which he knows is not to be done; damns himself to do, and dares better be damn'd than to do't.

SECOND LORD.

You do not know him, my lord, as we do; certain it is that he will steal himself into a man's favour, and for a week escape a great deal of discoveries, but when you find him out, you have him ever after.

BERTRAM.

Why, do you think he will make no deed at all of this, that so seriously he does address himself unto?

FIRST LORD.

None in the world; but return with an invention, and clap upon you two or three probable lies; but we have almost embossed him; you shall see his fall tonight; for indeed he is not for your lordship's respect.

SECOND LORD.

We'll make you some sport with the fox ere we case him. He was first smok'd by the old Lord Lafew; when his disguise and he is parted, tell me what a sprat you shall find him; which you shall see this very night.

FIRST LORD.

I must go look my twigs. He shall be caught.

BERTRAM.

Your brother, he shall go along with me.

FIRST LORD.

As't please your lordship. I'll leave you.

[Exit.]

BERTRAM.

Now will I lead you to the house, and show you

The lass I spoke of.

SECOND LORD.

But you say she's honest.

BERTRAM.

That's all the fault. I spoke with her but once,

And found her wondrous cold, but I sent to her

By this same coxcomb that we have i' the wind

Tokens and letters which she did re-send,

And this is all I have done. She's a fair creature;

Will you go see her?

SECOND LORD.

With all my heart, my lord.

[Exeunt.]

SCENE VII. Florence. A room in the Widow's house.

Enter Helena and Widow.

HELENA.

If you misdoubt me that I am not she,

I know not how I shall assure you further,

But I shall lose the grounds I work upon.

WIDOW.

Though my estate be fall'n, I was well born,

Nothing acquainted with these businesses,

And would not put my reputation now

In any staining act.

HELENA.

Nor would I wish you.

First give me trust, the count he is my husband,

And what to your sworn counsel I have spoken

Is so from word to word; and then you cannot,

By the good aid that I of you shall borrow,

Err in bestowing it.

WIDOW.

I should believe you,

For you have show'd me that which well approves

Y'are great in fortune.

HELENA.

Take this purse of gold,

And let me buy your friendly help thus far,

Which I will over-pay, and pay again

When I have found it. The count he woos your daughter

Lays down his wanton siege before her beauty,

Resolv'd to carry her; let her in fine consent,

As we'll direct her how 'tis best to bear it.

Now his important blood will naught deny

That she'll demand; a ring the county wears,

That downward hath succeeded in his house

From son to son, some four or five descents

Since the first father wore it. This ring he holds

In most rich choice; yet, in his idle fire,

To buy his will, it would not seem too dear,

Howe'er repented after.

WIDOW.

Now I see

The bottom of your purpose.

HELENA.

You see it lawful then; it is no more

But that your daughter, ere she seems as won,

Desires this ring; appoints him an encounter;

In fine, delivers me to fill the time,

Herself most chastely absent. After,

To marry her, I'll add three thousand crowns

To what is pass'd already.

WIDOW.

I have yielded.

Instruct my daughter how she shall persever,

That time and place with this deceit so lawful

May prove coherent. Every night he comes

With musics of all sorts, and songs compos'd

To her unworthiness: it nothing steads us

To chide him from our eaves; for he persists

As if his life lay on 't.

HELENA.

Why then tonight

Let us assay our plot; which, if it speed,

Is wicked meaning in a lawful deed,

And lawful meaning in a lawful act,

Where both not sin, and yet a sinful fact.

But let's about it.

[Exeunt.]

ACT IV.

SCENE I. Without the Florentine camp.

Enter first Lord with five or six Soldiers in ambush.

FIRST LORD.

He can come no other way but by this hedge-corner. When you sally upon him, speak what terrible language you will; though you understand it not yourselves, no matter; for we must not seem to understand him, unless someone among us, whom we must produce for an interpreter.

FIRST SOLDIER.

Good captain, let me be th' interpreter.

FIRST LORD.

Art not acquainted with him? Knows he not thy voice?

FIRST SOLDIER.

No sir, I warrant you.

FIRST LORD.

But what linsey-woolsey has thou to speak to us again?

FIRST SOLDIER.

E'en such as you speak to me.

FIRST LORD.

He must think us some band of strangers i' the adversary's entertainment. Now he hath a smack of all neighbouring languages, therefore we must every one be a man of his own fancy; not to know what we speak one to another, so we seem to know, is to know straight our purpose: choughs' language, gabble enough, and good enough. As for you, interpreter, you must seem very politic. But couch, ho! Here he comes; to beguile two hours in a sleep, and then to return and swear the lies he forges.

Enter Parolles.

PAROLLES.

Ten o'clock. Within these three hours 'twill be time enough to go home. What shall I say I have done? It must be a very plausive invention that carries it. They begin to smoke me, and disgraces have of late knock'd too often at my door. I find my tongue is too foolhardy, but my heart hath the fear of Mars before it, and of his creatures, not daring the reports of my tongue.

FIRST LORD.

[Aside.] This is the first truth that e'er thine own tongue was guilty of.

PAROLLES.

What the devil should move me to undertake the recovery of this drum, being not ignorant of the impossibility, and knowing I had no such purpose? I must give myself some hurts, and say I got them in exploit; yet slight ones will not carry it. They will say "Came you off with so little?" and great ones I dare not give. Wherefore, what's the instance? Tongue, I must put you into a butter-woman's mouth, and buy myself another of Bajazet's mule, if you prattle me into these perils.

FIRST LORD.

[Aside.] Is it possible he should know what he is, and be that he is?

PAROLLES.

I would the cutting of my garments would serve the turn, or the breaking of my Spanish sword.

FIRST LORD.

[Aside.] We cannot afford you so.

PAROLLES.

Or the baring of my beard, and to say it was in stratagem.

FIRST LORD.

[Aside.] 'Twould not do.

PAROLLES.

Or to drown my clothes, and say I was stripped.

FIRST LORD.

[Aside.] Hardly serve.

PAROLLES.

Though I swore I leap'd from the window of the citadel,—

FIRST LORD.

[Aside.] How deep?

PAROLLES.

Thirty fathom.

FIRST LORD.

[Aside.] Three great oaths would scarce make that be believed.

PAROLLES.

I would I had any drum of the enemy's; I would swear I recover'd it.

FIRST LORD.

[Aside.] You shall hear one anon.

PAROLLES.

A drum now of the enemy's!

[Alarum within.]

FIRST LORD.

Throca movousus, cargo, cargo, cargo.

ALL.

Cargo, cargo, cargo, villianda par corbo, cargo.

[They seize and blindfold him.]

PAROLLES.

O, ransom, ransom! Do not hide mine eyes.

FIRST SOLDIER.

Boskos thromuldo boskos.

PAROLLES.

I know you are the Muskos' regiment,

And I shall lose my life for want of language.

If there be here German, or Dane, Low Dutch,

Italian, or French, let him speak to me,

I'll discover that which shall undo the Florentine.

FIRST SOLDIER.

Boskos vauvado. I understand thee, and can speak thy tongue. Kerelybonto. Sir, Betake thee to thy faith, for seventeen poniards are at thy bosom.

PAROLLES.

O!

FIRST SOLDIER.

O, pray, pray, pray!

Manka revania dulche.

FIRST LORD.

Oscorbidulchos volivorco.

FIRST SOLDIER.

The General is content to spare thee yet;

And, hoodwink'd as thou art, will lead thee on

To gather from thee. Haply thou mayst inform

Something to save thy life.

PAROLLES.

O, let me live,

And all the secrets of our camp I'll show,

Their force, their purposes; nay, I'll speak that

Which you will wonder at.

FIRST SOLDIER.

But wilt thou faithfully?

PAROLLES.

If I do not, damn me.

FIRST SOLDIER.

Acordo linta.

Come on; thou art granted space.

[Exit, with Parolles guarded.]

A short alarum within.

FIRST LORD.

Go tell the Count Rossillon and my brother

We have caught the woodcock, and will keep him muffled

Till we do hear from them.

SECOND SOLDIER.

Captain, I will.

FIRST LORD.

'A will betray us all unto ourselves;

Inform on that.

SECOND SOLDIER.

So I will, sir.

FIRST LORD.

Till then I'll keep him dark, and safely lock'd.

[Exeunt.]

SCENE II. Florence. A room in the Widow's house.

Enter Bertram and Diana.

BERTRAM.

They told me that your name was Fontybell.

DIANA.

No, my good lord, Diana.

BERTRAM.

Titled goddess;

And worth it, with addition! But, fair soul,

In your fine frame hath love no quality?

If the quick fire of youth light not your mind,

You are no maiden but a monument;

When you are dead, you should be such a one

As you are now; for you are cold and stern,

And now you should be as your mother was

When your sweet self was got.

DIANA.

She then was honest.

BERTRAM.

So should you be.

DIANA.

No.

My mother did but duty; such, my lord,

As you owe to your wife.

BERTRAM.

No more a' that!

I pr'ythee do not strive against my vows;

I was compell'd to her; but I love thee

By love's own sweet constraint, and will for ever

Do thee all rights of service.

DIANA.

Ay, so you serve us

Till we serve you; but when you have our roses,

You barely leave our thorns to prick ourselves,

And mock us with our bareness.

BERTRAM.

How have I sworn?

DIANA.

'Tis not the many oaths that makes the truth,

But the plain single vow that is vow'd true.

What is not holy, that we swear not by,

But take the highest to witness: then, pray you, tell me,

If I should swear by Jove's great attributes

I lov'd you dearly, would you believe my oaths

When I did love you ill? This has no holding,

To swear by him whom I protest to love

That I will work against him. Therefore your oaths

Are words and poor conditions; but unseal'd,—

At least in my opinion.

BERTRAM.

Change it, change it.

Be not so holy-cruel. Love is holy;

And my integrity ne'er knew the crafts

That you do charge men with. Stand no more off,

But give thyself unto my sick desires,

Who then recovers. Say thou art mine, and ever

My love as it begins shall so persever.

DIANA.

I see that men make hopes in such a case,

That we'll forsake ourselves. Give me that ring.

BERTRAM.

I'll lend it thee, my dear, but have no power

To give it from me.

DIANA.

Will you not, my lord?

BERTRAM.

It is an honour 'longing to our house,

Bequeathed down from many ancestors,

Which were the greatest obloquy i' the world

In me to lose.

DIANA.

Mine honour's such a ring;

My chastity's the jewel of our house,

Bequeathed down from many ancestors,

Which were the greatest obloquy i' the world

In me to lose. Thus your own proper wisdom

Brings in the champion honour on my part

Against your vain assault.

BERTRAM.

Here, take my ring;

My house, mine honour, yea, my life be thine,

And I'll be bid by thee.

DIANA.

When midnight comes, knock at my chamber window;

I'll order take my mother shall not hear.

Now will I charge you in the band of truth,

When you have conquer'd my yet maiden-bed,

Remain there but an hour, nor speak to me.

My reasons are most strong; and you shall know them

When back again this ring shall be deliver'd;

And on your finger in the night, I'll put

Another ring, that what in time proceeds

May token to the future our past deeds.

Adieu till then; then fail not. You have won

A wife of me, though there my hope be done.

BERTRAM.

A heaven on earth I have won by wooing thee.

[Exit.]

DIANA.

For which live long to thank both heaven and me!

You may so in the end.

My mother told me just how he would woo,

As if she sat in's heart. She says all men

Have the like oaths. He had sworn to marry me

When his wife's dead; therefore I'll lie with him

When I am buried. Since Frenchmen are so braid,

Marry that will, I live and die a maid.

Only, in this disguise, I think't no sin

To cozen him that would unjustly win.

[Exit.]

SCENE III. The Florentine camp.

Enter the two French Lords and two or three Soldiers.

FIRST LORD.

You have not given him his mother's letter?

SECOND LORD.

I have deliv'red it an hour since; there is something in't that stings his nature; for on the reading it, he chang'd almost into another man.

FIRST LORD.

He has much worthy blame laid upon him for shaking off so good a wife and so sweet a lady.

SECOND LORD.

Especially he hath incurred the everlasting displeasure of the king, who had even tun'd his bounty to sing happiness to him. I will tell you a thing, but you shall let it dwell darkly with you.

FIRST LORD.

When you have spoken it, 'tis dead, and I am the grave of it.

SECOND LORD.

He hath perverted a young gentlewoman here in Florence, of a most chaste renown, and this night he fleshes his will in the spoil of her honour; he hath given her his monumental ring, and thinks himself made in the unchaste composition.

FIRST LORD.

Now, God delay our rebellion! As we are ourselves, what things are we!

SECOND LORD.

Merely our own traitors. And as in the common course of all treasons, we still see them reveal themselves till they attain to their abhorr'd ends; so he that in this action contrives against his own nobility, in his proper stream, o'erflows himself.

FIRST LORD.

Is it not meant damnable in us to be trumpeters of our unlawful intents? We shall not then have his company tonight?

SECOND LORD.

Not till after midnight; for he is dieted to his hour.

FIRST LORD.

That approaches apace. I would gladly have him see his company anatomized, that he might take a measure of his own judgments, wherein so curiously he had set this counterfeit.

SECOND LORD.

We will not meddle with him till he come; for his presence must be the whip of the other.

FIRST LORD.

In the meantime, what hear you of these wars?

SECOND LORD.

I hear there is an overture of peace.

FIRST LORD.

Nay, I assure you, a peace concluded.

SECOND LORD.

What will Count Rossillon do then? Will he travel higher, or return again into France?

FIRST LORD.

I perceive by this demand, you are not altogether of his council.

SECOND LORD.

Let it be forbid, sir! So should I be a great deal of his act.

FIRST LORD.

Sir, his wife some two months since fled from his house. Her pretence is a pilgrimage to Saint Jaques le Grand; which holy undertaking with most austere sanctimony she accomplished; and there residing, the tenderness of her nature became as a prey to her grief; in fine, made a groan of her last breath, and now she sings in heaven.

SECOND LORD.

How is this justified?

FIRST LORD.

The stronger part of it by her own letters, which makes her story true, even to the point of her death. Her death itself, which could not be her office to say is come, was faithfully confirm'd by the rector of the place.

SECOND LORD.

Hath the count all this intelligence?

FIRST LORD.

Ay, and the particular confirmations, point from point, to the full arming of the verity.

SECOND LORD.

I am heartily sorry that he'll be glad of this.

FIRST LORD.

How mightily sometimes we make us comforts of our losses!

SECOND LORD.

And how mightily some other times we drown our gain in tears! The great dignity that his valour hath here acquir'd for him shall at home be encountered with a shame as ample.

FIRST LORD.

The web of our life is of a mingled yarn, good and ill together; our virtues would be proud if our faults whipped them not; and our crimes would despair if they were not cherish'd by our virtues.

Enter a Messenger.

How now? Where's your master?

MESSENGER.

He met the duke in the street, sir; of whom he hath taken a solemn leave: his lordship will next morning for France. The duke hath offered him letters of commendations to the king.

SECOND LORD.

They shall be no more than needful there, if they were more than they can commend.

Enter Bertram.

FIRST LORD.

They cannot be too sweet for the king's tartness. Here's his lordship now. How now, my lord, is't not after midnight?

BERTRAM.

I have tonight despatch'd sixteen businesses, a month's length apiece; by an abstract of success: I have congied with the duke, done my adieu with his nearest; buried a wife, mourn'd for her, writ to my lady mother I am returning, entertained my convoy, and between these main parcels of despatch effected many nicer needs: the last was the greatest, but that I have not ended yet.

SECOND LORD.

If the business be of any difficulty and this morning your departure hence, it requires haste of your lordship.

BERTRAM.

I mean the business is not ended, as fearing to hear of it hereafter. But shall we have this dialogue between the Fool and the Soldier? Come, bring forth this counterfeit module has deceiv'd me like a double-meaning prophesier.

SECOND LORD.

Bring him forth.

[Exeunt Soldiers.]

Has sat i' the stocks all night, poor gallant knave.

BERTRAM.

No matter; his heels have deserv'd it, in usurping his spurs so long. How does he carry himself?

FIRST LORD.

I have told your lordship already; the stocks carry him. But to answer you as you would be understood: he weeps like a wench that had shed her milk; he hath confessed himself to Morgan, whom he supposes to be a friar, from the time of his remembrance to this very instant disaster of his setting i' the stocks. And what think you he hath confessed?

BERTRAM.

Nothing of me, has he?

SECOND LORD.

His confession is taken, and it shall be read to his face; if your lordship be in't, as I believe you are, you must have the patience to hear it.

Enter Soldiers with Parolles.

BERTRAM.

A plague upon him! muffled! he can say nothing of me; hush, hush!

FIRST LORD.

Hoodman comes! Portotartarossa.

FIRST SOLDIER.

He calls for the tortures. What will you say without 'em?

PAROLLES.

I will confess what I know without constraint. If ye pinch me like a pasty I can say no more.

FIRST SOLDIER.

Bosko chimurcho.

FIRST LORD.

Boblibindo chicurmurco.

FIRST SOLDIER.

You are a merciful general. Our general bids you answer to what I shall ask you out of a note.

PAROLLES.

And truly, as I hope to live.

FIRST SOLDIER.

'First demand of him how many horse the duke is strong.' What say you to that?

PAROLLES.

Five or six thousand; but very weak and unserviceable: the troops are all scattered, and the commanders very poor rogues, upon my reputation and credit, and as I hope to live.

FIRST SOLDIER.

Shall I set down your answer so?

PAROLLES.

Do. I'll take the sacrament on 't, how and which way you will.

BERTRAM.

All's one to him. What a past-saving slave is this!

FIRST LORD.

You are deceived, my lord; this is Monsieur Parolles, the gallant militarist (that was his own phrase), that had the whole theoric of war in the knot of his scarf, and the practice in the chape of his dagger.

SECOND LORD.

I will never trust a man again for keeping his sword clean, nor believe he can have everything in him by wearing his apparel neatly.

FIRST SOLDIER.

Well, that's set down.

PAROLLES.

'Five or six thousand horse' I said—I will say true—or thereabouts, set down,—for I'll speak truth.

FIRST LORD.

He's very near the truth in this.

BERTRAM.

But I con him no thanks for't in the nature he delivers it.

PAROLLES.

Poor rogues, I pray you say.

FIRST SOLDIER.

Well, that's set down.

PAROLLES.

I humbly thank you, sir; a truth's a truth, the rogues are marvellous poor.

FIRST SOLDIER.

'Demand of him of what strength they are a-foot.' What say you to that?

PAROLLES.

By my troth, sir, if I were to live this present hour, I will tell true. Let me see: Spurio, a hundred and fifty, Sebastian, so many; Corambus, so many; Jaques, so many; Guiltian, Cosmo, Lodowick, and Gratii, two hundred fifty each; mine own company, Chitopher, Vaumond, Bentii, two hundred fifty each: so that the muster-file, rotten and sound, upon my life, amounts not to fifteen thousand poll; half of the which dare not shake the snow from off their cassocks lest they shake themselves to pieces.

BERTRAM.

What shall be done to him?

FIRST LORD.

Nothing, but let him have thanks. Demand of him my condition, and what credit I have with the duke.

FIRST SOLDIER.

Well, that's set down. 'You shall demand of him whether one Captain Dumaine be i' the camp, a Frenchman; what his reputation is with the duke, what his valour, honesty and expertness in wars; or whether he thinks it were not possible with well-weighing sums of gold to corrupt him to a revolt.' What say you to this? What do you know of it?

PAROLLES.

I beseech you, let me answer to the particular of the inter'gatories. Demand them singly.

FIRST SOLDIER.

Do you know this Captain Dumaine?

PAROLLES.

I know him: he was a botcher's 'prentice in Paris, from whence he was whipped for getting the shrieve's fool with child, a dumb innocent that could not say him nay.

[First Lord lifts up his hand in anger.]

BERTRAM.

Nay, by your leave, hold your hands; though I know his brains are forfeit to the next tile that falls.

FIRST SOLDIER.

Well, is this captain in the Duke of Florence's camp?

PAROLLES.

Upon my knowledge, he is, and lousy.

FIRST LORD.

Nay, look not so upon me; we shall hear of your lordship anon.

FIRST SOLDIER.

What is his reputation with the duke?

PAROLLES.

The duke knows him for no other but a poor officer of mine, and writ to me this other day to turn him out o' the band. I think I have his letter in my pocket.

FIRST SOLDIER.

Marry, we'll search.

PAROLLES.

In good sadness, I do not know; either it is there or it is upon a file, with the duke's other letters, in my tent.

FIRST SOLDIER.

Here 'tis; here's a paper; shall I read it to you?

PAROLLES.

I do not know if it be it or no.

BERTRAM.

Our interpreter does it well.

FIRST LORD.

Excellently.

FIRST SOLDIER.

[Reads.] Dian, the Count's a fool, and full of gold.

PAROLLES.

That is not the duke's letter, sir; that is an advertisement to a proper maid in Florence, one Diana, to take heed of the allurement of one Count Rossillon, a foolish idle boy, but for all that very ruttish. I pray you, sir, put it up again.

FIRST SOLDIER.

Nay, I'll read it first by your favour.

PAROLLES.

My meaning in't, I protest, was very honest in the behalf of the maid; for I knew the young count to be a dangerous and lascivious boy, who is a whale to virginity, and devours up all the fry it finds.

BERTRAM.

Damnable both sides rogue!

FIRST SOLDIER.

[Reads.]

When he swears oaths, bid him drop gold, and take it;

After he scores, he never pays the score.

Half won is match well made; match, and well make it;

He ne'er pays after-debts, take it before.

And say a soldier, 'Dian,' told thee this:

Men are to mell with, boys are not to kiss;

For count of this, the count's a fool, I know it,

Who pays before, but not when he does owe it.

Thine, as he vow'd to thee in thine ear,

PAROLLES.

BERTRAM.

He shall be whipped through the army with this rhyme in's forehead.

SECOND LORD.

This is your devoted friend, sir, the manifold linguist, and the armipotent soldier.

BERTRAM.

I could endure anything before but a cat, and now he's a cat to me.

FIRST SOLDIER.

I perceive, sir, by our general's looks we shall be fain to hang you.

PAROLLES.

My life, sir, in any case. Not that I am afraid to die, but that, my offences being many, I would repent out the remainder of nature. Let me live, sir, in a dungeon, i' the stocks, or anywhere, so I may live.

FIRST SOLDIER.

We'll see what may be done, so you confess freely. Therefore, once more to this Captain Dumaine: you have answer'd to his reputation with the duke, and to his valour. What is his honesty?

PAROLLES.

He will steal, sir, an egg out of a cloister: for rapes and ravishments he parallels Nessus. He professes not keeping of oaths; in breaking them he is stronger than Hercules. He will lie, sir, with such volubility that you would think truth were a fool: drunkenness is his best virtue, for he will be swine-drunk, and in his sleep he does little harm, save to his bedclothes about him; but they know his conditions and lay him in straw. I have but little more to say, sir, of his honesty; he has everything that an honest man should not have; what an honest man should have, he has nothing.

FIRST LORD.

I begin to love him for this.

BERTRAM.

For this description of thine honesty? A pox upon him for me, he's more and more a cat.

FIRST SOLDIER.

What say you to his expertness in war?

PAROLLES.

Faith, sir, has led the drum before the English tragedians,—to belie him I will not,—and more of his soldiership I know not, except in that country he had the honour to be the officer at a place there called Mile-end, to instruct for the doubling of files. I would do the man what honour I can, but of this I am not certain.

FIRST LORD.

He hath out-villain'd villainy so far that the rarity redeems him.

BERTRAM.

A pox on him! He's a cat still.

FIRST SOLDIER.

His qualities being at this poor price, I need not to ask you if gold will corrupt him to revolt.

PAROLLES.

Sir, for a quart d'ecu he will sell the fee-simple of his salvation, the inheritance of it, and cut the entail from all remainders, and a perpetual succession for it perpetually.

FIRST SOLDIER.

What's his brother, the other Captain Dumaine?

SECOND LORD.

Why does he ask him of me?

FIRST SOLDIER.

What's he?

PAROLLES.

E'en a crow o' the same nest; not altogether so great as the first in goodness, but greater a great deal in evil. He excels his brother for a coward, yet his brother is reputed one of the best that is. In a retreat he outruns any lackey; marry, in coming on he has the cramp.

FIRST SOLDIER.

If your life be saved, will you undertake to betray the Florentine?

PAROLLES.

Ay, and the captain of his horse, Count Rossillon.

FIRST SOLDIER.

I'll whisper with the general, and know his pleasure.

PAROLLES.

[Aside.] I'll no more drumming; a plague of all drums! Only to seem to deserve well, and to beguile the supposition of that lascivious young boy the count, have I run into this danger: yet who would have suspected an ambush where I was taken?

FIRST SOLDIER.

There is no remedy, sir, but you must die. The general says you that have so traitorously discovered the secrets of your army, and made such pestiferous reports of men very nobly held, can serve the world for no honest use; therefore you must die. Come, headsman, off with his head.

PAROLLES.

O Lord! sir, let me live, or let me see my death.

FIRST SOLDIER.

That shall you, and take your leave of all your friends.

[Unmuffling him.]

So, look about you; know you any here?

BERTRAM.

Good morrow, noble captain.

SECOND LORD.

God bless you, Captain Parolles.

FIRST LORD.

God save you, noble captain.

SECOND LORD.

Captain, what greeting will you to my Lord Lafew? I am for France.

FIRST LORD.

Good Captain, will you give me a copy of the sonnet you writ to Diana in behalf of the Count Rossillon? And I were not a very coward I'd compel it of you; but fare you well.

[Exeunt Bertram, Lords &c.]

FIRST SOLDIER.

You are undone, captain: all but your scarf; that has a knot on't yet.

PAROLLES.

Who cannot be crushed with a plot?

FIRST SOLDIER.

If you could find out a country where but women were that had received so much shame, you might begin an impudent nation. Fare ye well, sir. I am for France too; we shall speak of you there.

[Exeunt.]

PAROLLES.

Yet am I thankful. If my heart were great

'Twould burst at this. Captain I'll be no more,

But I will eat, and drink, and sleep as soft

As captain shall. Simply the thing I am

Shall make me live. Who knows himself a braggart,

Let him fear this; for it will come to pass

That every braggart shall be found an ass.

Rust, sword; cool, blushes; and, Parolles live

Safest in shame; being fool'd, by foolery thrive.

There's place and means for every man alive.

I'll after them.

[Exit.]

SCENE IV. Florence. A room in the Widow's house.

Enter Helena, Widow and Diana.

HELENA.

That you may well perceive I have not wrong'd you

One of the greatest in the Christian world

Shall be my surety; fore whose throne 'tis needful,

Ere I can perfect mine intents, to kneel.

Time was I did him a desired office,

Dear almost as his life; which gratitude

Through flinty Tartar's bosom would peep forth,

And answer thanks. I duly am inform'd

His grace is at Marseilles; to which place

We have convenient convoy. You must know

I am supposed dead. The army breaking,

My husband hies him home, where, heaven aiding,

And by the leave of my good lord the king,

We'll be before our welcome.

WIDOW.

Gentle madam,

You never had a servant to whose trust

Your business was more welcome.

HELENA.

Nor you, mistress,

Ever a friend whose thoughts more truly labour

To recompense your love. Doubt not but heaven

Hath brought me up to be your daughter's dower,

As it hath fated her to be my motive

And helper to a husband. But, O strange men!

That can such sweet use make of what they hate,

When saucy trusting of the cozen'd thoughts

Defiles the pitchy night; so lust doth play

With what it loathes, for that which is away.

But more of this hereafter. You, Diana,

Under my poor instructions yet must suffer

Something in my behalf.

DIANA.

Let death and honesty

Go with your impositions, I am yours

Upon your will to suffer.

HELENA.

Yet, I pray you;

But with the word the time will bring on summer,

When briers shall have leaves as well as thorns,

And be as sweet as sharp. We must away;

Our waggon is prepar'd, and time revives us.

All's well that ends well; still the fine's the crown.

Whate'er the course, the end is the renown.

[Exeunt.]

SCENE V. Rossillon. A room in the Countess's palace.

Enter Clown, Countess and Lafew.

LAFEW.

No, no, no, your son was misled with a snipt-taffeta fellow there, whose villanous saffron would have made all the unbak'd and doughy youth of a nation in his colour. Your daughter-in-law had been alive at this hour, and your son here at home, more advanc'd by the king than by that red-tail'd humble-bee I speak of.

COUNTESS.

I would I had not known him; it was the death of the most virtuous gentlewoman that ever nature had praise for creating. If she had partaken of my flesh and cost me the dearest groans of a mother, I could not have owed her a more rooted love.

LAFEW.

'Twas a good lady, 'twas a good lady. We may pick a thousand salads ere we light on such another herb.

CLOWN.

Indeed, sir, she was the sweet marjoram of the salad, or, rather, the herb of grace.

LAFEW.

They are not herbs, you knave; they are nose-herbs.

CLOWN.

I am no great Nebuchadnezzar, sir; I have not much skill in grass.

LAFEW.

Whether dost thou profess thyself,—a knave or a fool?

CLOWN.

A fool, sir, at a woman's service, and a knave at a man's.

LAFEW.

Your distinction?

CLOWN.

I would cozen the man of his wife, and do his service.

LAFEW.

So you were a knave at his service indeed.

CLOWN.

And I would give his wife my bauble, sir, to do her service.

LAFEW.

I will subscribe for thee; thou art both knave and fool.

CLOWN.

At your service.

LAFEW.

No, no, no.

CLOWN.

Why, sir, if I cannot serve you, I can serve as great a prince as you are.

LAFEW.

Who's that? a Frenchman?

CLOWN.

Faith, sir, 'a has an English name; but his phisnomy is more hotter in France than there.

306

LAFEW.

What prince is that?

CLOWN.

The black prince, sir; alias the prince of darkness; alias the devil.

LAFEW.

Hold thee, there's my purse. I give thee not this to suggest thee from thy master thou talk'st of; serve him still.

CLOWN.

I am a woodland fellow, sir, that always loved a great fire, and the master I speak of ever keeps a good fire. But sure he is the prince of the world; let his nobility remain in's court. I am for the house with the narrow gate, which I take to be too little for pomp to enter: some that humble themselves may, but the many will be too chill and tender, and they'll be for the flow'ry way that leads to the broad gate and the great fire.

LAFEW.

Go thy ways, I begin to be a-weary of thee; and I tell thee so before, because I would not fall out with thee. Go thy ways; let my horses be well look'd to, without any tricks.

CLOWN.

If I put any tricks upon 'em, sir, they shall be jades' tricks, which are their own right by the law of nature.

[Exit.]

LAFEW.

A shrewd knave, and an unhappy.

COUNTESS.

So he is. My lord that's gone made himself much sport out of him; by his authority he remains here, which he thinks is a patent for his sauciness;

and indeed he has no pace, but runs where he will.

LAFEW.

I like him well; 'tis not amiss. And I was about to tell you, since I heard of the good lady's death, and that my lord your son was upon his return home, I moved the king my master to speak in the behalf of my daughter; which, in the minority of them both, his majesty out of a self-gracious remembrance did first propose. His highness hath promis'd me to do it; and, to stop up the displeasure he hath conceived against your son, there is no fitter matter. How does your ladyship like it?

COUNTESS.

With very much content, my lord, and I wish it happily effected.

LAFEW.

His highness comes post from Marseilles, of as able body as when he number'd thirty; he will be here tomorrow, or I am deceived by him that in such intelligence hath seldom fail'd.

COUNTESS.

It rejoices me that I hope I shall see him ere I die. I have letters that my son will be here tonight. I shall beseech your lordship to remain with me till they meet together.

LAFEW.

Madam, I was thinking with what manners I might safely be admitted.

COUNTESS.

You need but plead your honourable privilege.

LAFEW.

Lady, of that I have made a bold charter; but, I thank my God, it holds yet.

Enter Clown.

CLOWN.

O madam, yonder's my lord your son with a patch of velvet on's face; whether there be a scar under't or no, the velvet knows; but 'tis a goodly patch of velvet. His left cheek is a cheek of two pile and a half, but his right cheek is worn bare.

LAFEW.

A scar nobly got, or a noble scar, is a good livery of honour; so belike is that.

CLOWN.

But it is your carbonado'd face.

LAFEW.

Let us go see your son, I pray you. I long to talk with the young noble soldier.

CLOWN.

Faith, there's a dozen of 'em, with delicate fine hats, and most courteous feathers, which bow the head and nod at every man.

[Exeunt.]

ACT V.

SCENE I. Marseilles. A street.

Enter Helena, Widow and Diana with two Attendants.

HELENA.

But this exceeding posting day and night

Must wear your spirits low. We cannot help it.

But since you have made the days and nights as one,

To wear your gentle limbs in my affairs,

Be bold you do so grow in my requital

As nothing can unroot you. In happy time;—

Enter a Gentleman.

This man may help me to his majesty's ear,

If he would spend his power. God save you, sir.

GENTLEMAN.

And you.

HELENA.

Sir, I have seen you in the court of France.

GENTLEMAN.

I have been sometimes there.

HELENA.

I do presume, sir, that you are not fallen

From the report that goes upon your goodness;

And therefore, goaded with most sharp occasions,

Which lay nice manners by, I put you to

The use of your own virtues, for the which

I shall continue thankful.

GENTLEMAN.

What's your will?

HELENA.

That it will please you

To give this poor petition to the king,

And aid me with that store of power you have

To come into his presence.

GENTLEMAN.

The king's not here.

HELENA.

Not here, sir?

GENTLEMAN.

Not indeed.

He hence remov'd last night, and with more haste

Than is his use.

WIDOW.

Lord, how we lose our pains!

HELENA.

All's well that ends well yet,

Though time seem so adverse and means unfit.

I do beseech you, whither is he gone?

GENTLEMAN.

Marry, as I take it, to Rossillon;

Whither I am going.

HELENA.

I do beseech you, sir,

Since you are like to see the king before me,

Commend the paper to his gracious hand,

Which I presume shall render you no blame,

But rather make you thank your pains for it.

I will come after you with what good speed

Our means will make us means.

GENTLEMAN.

This I'll do for you.

HELENA.

And you shall find yourself to be well thank'd,

Whate'er falls more. We must to horse again.

Go, go, provide.

[Exeunt.]

SCENE II. Rossillon. The inner court of the Countess's palace.

Enter Clown and Parolles.

PAROLLES.

Good Monsieur Lavache, give my Lord Lafew this letter; I have ere now, sir, been better known to you, when I have held familiarity with fresher clothes; but I am now, sir, muddied in Fortune's mood, and smell somewhat strong of her strong displeasure.

CLOWN.

Truly, Fortune's displeasure is but sluttish, if it smell so strongly as thou speak'st of. I will henceforth eat no fish of Fortune's buttering. Pr'ythee, allow the wind.

PAROLLES.

Nay, you need not to stop your nose, sir. I spake but by a metaphor.

CLOWN.

Indeed, sir, if your metaphor stink, I will stop my nose, or against any man's metaphor. Pr'ythee, get thee further.

PAROLLES.

Pray you, sir, deliver me this paper.

CLOWN.

Foh, pr'ythee stand away. A paper from Fortune's close-stool to give to a nobleman! Look here he comes himself.

Enter Lafew.

Here is a pur of Fortune's, sir, or of Fortune's cat, but not a musk-cat, that has fallen into the unclean fishpond of her displeasure, and as he says, is muddied withal. Pray you, sir, use the carp as you may, for he looks like a poor, decayed, ingenious, foolish, rascally knave. I do pity his distress in my similes of comfort, and leave him to your lordship.

[Exit.]

PAROLLES.

My lord, I am a man whom Fortune hath cruelly scratch'd.

LAFEW.

And what would you have me to do? 'Tis too late to pare her nails now. Wherein have you played the knave with Fortune that she should scratch you, who of herself is a good lady, and would not have knaves thrive long under her? There's a quart d'ecu for you. Let the justices make you and Fortune friends; I am for other business.

PAROLLES.

I beseech your honour to hear me one single word.

LAFEW.

You beg a single penny more. Come, you shall ha't; save your word.

PAROLLES.

My name, my good lord, is Parolles.

LAFEW.

You beg more than word then. Cox my passion! Give me your hand. How does your drum?

PAROLLES.

O my good lord, you were the first that found me.

LAFEW.

Was I, in sooth? And I was the first that lost thee.

PAROLLES.

It lies in you, my lord, to bring me in some grace, for you did bring me out.

LAFEW.

Out upon thee, knave! dost thou put upon me at once both the office of God and the devil? One brings the in grace, and the other brings thee out.

[Trumpets sound.]

The king's coming; I know by his trumpets. Sirrah, inquire further after me. I had talk of you last night; though you are a fool and a knave, you shall eat. Go to; follow.

PAROLLES.

I praise God for you.

[Exeunt.]

SCENE III. The same. A room in the Countess's palace.

Flourish. Enter King, Countess, Lafew, Lords, Gentlemen, Guards &c.

KING.

We lost a jewel of her, and our esteem

Was made much poorer by it; but your son,

As mad in folly, lack'd the sense to know

Her estimation home.

COUNTESS.

'Tis past, my liege,

And I beseech your majesty to make it

Natural rebellion, done i' the blaze of youth,

When oil and fire, too strong for reason's force,

O'erbears it and burns on.

KING.

My honour'd lady,

I have forgiven and forgotten all,

Though my revenges were high bent upon him,

And watch'd the time to shoot.

LAFEW.

This I must say,—

But first, I beg my pardon,—the young lord

Did to his majesty, his mother, and his lady,

Offence of mighty note; but to himself

The greatest wrong of all. He lost a wife

Whose beauty did astonish the survey

Of richest eyes; whose words all ears took captive;

Whose dear perfection hearts that scorn'd to serve

Humbly call'd mistress.

KING.

Praising what is lost

Makes the remembrance dear. Well, call him hither;

We are reconcil'd, and the first view shall kill

All repetition. Let him not ask our pardon;

The nature of his great offence is dead,

And deeper than oblivion do we bury

Th' incensing relics of it. Let him approach

A stranger, no offender; and inform him

So 'tis our will he should.

GENTLEMAN.

I shall, my liege.

[Exit Gentleman.]

KING.

What says he to your daughter? Have you spoke?

LAFEW.

All that he is hath reference to your highness.

KING.

Then shall we have a match. I have letters sent me

That sets him high in fame.

Enter Bertram.

LAFEW.

He looks well on 't.

KING.

I am not a day of season,

For thou mayst see a sunshine and a hail

In me at once. But to the brightest beams

Distracted clouds give way; so stand thou forth;

The time is fair again.

BERTRAM.

My high-repented blames

Dear sovereign, pardon to me.

KING.

All is whole.

Not one word more of the consumed time.

Let's take the instant by the forward top;

For we are old, and on our quick'st decrees

Th'inaudible and noiseless foot of time

Steals ere we can effect them. You remember

The daughter of this lord?

BERTRAM.

Admiringly, my liege. At first

I stuck my choice upon her, ere my heart

Durst make too bold herald of my tongue:

Where the impression of mine eye infixing,

Contempt his scornful perspective did lend me,

Which warp'd the line of every other favour,

Scorn'd a fair colour, or express'd it stolen,

Extended or contracted all proportions

To a most hideous object. Thence it came

That she whom all men prais'd, and whom myself,

Since I have lost, have lov'd, was in mine eye

The dust that did offend it.

KING.

Well excus'd:

That thou didst love her, strikes some scores away

From the great compt: but love that comes too late,

Like a remorseful pardon slowly carried,

To the great sender turns a sour offence,

Crying, That's good that's gone. Our rash faults

Make trivial price of serious things we have,

Not knowing them until we know their grave.

Oft our displeasures, to ourselves unjust,

Destroy our friends, and after weep their dust:

Our own love waking cries to see what's done,

While shameful hate sleeps out the afternoon.

Be this sweet Helen's knell, and now forget her.

Send forth your amorous token for fair Maudlin.

The main consents are had, and here we'll stay

To see our widower's second marriage-day.

COUNTESS.

Which better than the first, O dear heaven, bless!

Or, ere they meet, in me, O nature, cesse!

LAFEW.

Come on, my son, in whom my house's name

Must be digested; give a favour from you,

To sparkle in the spirits of my daughter,

That she may quickly come.

> [Bertram gives a ring to Lafew.]

By my old beard,

And ev'ry hair that's on 't, Helen that's dead

Was a sweet creature: such a ring as this,

The last that e'er I took her leave at court,

I saw upon her finger.

BERTRAM.

Hers it was not.

KING.

Now, pray you, let me see it; for mine eye,

While I was speaking, oft was fasten'd to it.

This ring was mine; and when I gave it Helen

I bade her, if her fortunes ever stood

Necessitied to help, that by this token

I would relieve her. Had you that craft to 'reave her

Of what should stead her most?

BERTRAM.

My gracious sovereign,

Howe'er it pleases you to take it so,

The ring was never hers.

COUNTESS.

Son, on my life,

I have seen her wear it; and she reckon'd it

At her life's rate.

LAFEW.

I am sure I saw her wear it.

BERTRAM.

You are deceiv'd, my lord; she never saw it.

In Florence was it from a casement thrown me,

Wrapp'd in a paper, which contain'd the name

Of her that threw it. Noble she was, and thought

I stood engag'd; but when I had subscrib'd

To mine own fortune, and inform'd her fully

I could not answer in that course of honour

As she had made the overture, she ceas'd,

In heavy satisfaction, and would never

Receive the ring again.

KING.

Plutus himself,

That knows the tinct and multiplying medicine,

Hath not in nature's mystery more science

Than I have in this ring. 'Twas mine, 'twas Helen's,

Whoever gave it you. Then if you know

That you are well acquainted with yourself,

Confess 'twas hers, and by what rough enforcement

You got it from her. She call'd the saints to surety

That she would never put it from her finger

Unless she gave it to yourself in bed,

Where you have never come, or sent it us

Upon her great disaster.

BERTRAM.

She never saw it.

KING.

Thou speak'st it falsely, as I love mine honour,

And mak'st conjectural fears to come into me

Which I would fain shut out. If it should prove

That thou art so inhuman,—'twill not prove so:

And yet I know not, thou didst hate her deadly.

And she is dead; which nothing but to close

Her eyes myself, could win me to believe

More than to see this ring. Take him away.

[Guards seize Bertram.]

My fore-past proofs, howe'er the matter fall,

Shall tax my fears of little vanity,

Having vainly fear'd too little. Away with him.

We'll sift this matter further.

BERTRAM.

If you shall prove

This ring was ever hers, you shall as easy

Prove that I husbanded her bed in Florence,

Where she yet never was.

[Exit, guarded.]

KING.

I am wrapp'd in dismal thinkings.

Enter a Gentleman.

GENTLEMAN.

Gracious sovereign,

Whether I have been to blame or no, I know not:

Here's a petition from a Florentine,

Who hath for four or five removes come short

To tender it herself. I undertook it,

Vanquish'd thereto by the fair grace and speech

Of the poor suppliant, who by this, I know,

Is here attending: her business looks in her

With an importing visage, and she told me

In a sweet verbal brief, it did concern

Your highness with herself.

KING.

[Reads.] Upon his many protestations to marry me when his wife was dead, I blush to say it, he won me. Now is the Count Rossillon a widower; his vows are forfeited to me, and my honour's paid to him. He stole from Florence, taking no leave, and I follow him to his country for justice. Grant it me, O king, in you it best lies; otherwise a seducer flourishes, and a poor maid is undone.

DIANA CAPILET.

LAFEW.

I will buy me a son-in-law in a fair, and toll for this. I'll none of him.

KING.

The heavens have thought well on thee, Lafew,

To bring forth this discovery. Seek these suitors.

Go speedily, and bring again the count.

[Exeunt Gentleman and some Attendants.]

I am afeard the life of Helen, lady,

324

Was foully snatch'd.

COUNTESS.

Now, justice on the doers!

Enter Bertram, guarded.

KING.

I wonder, sir, since wives are monsters to you,

And that you fly them as you swear them lordship,

Yet you desire to marry. What woman's that?

Enter Widow and Diana.

DIANA.

I am, my lord, a wretched Florentine,

Derived from the ancient Capilet;

My suit, as I do understand, you know,

And therefore know how far I may be pitied.

WIDOW.

I am her mother, sir, whose age and honour

Both suffer under this complaint we bring,

And both shall cease, without your remedy.

KING.

Come hither, count; do you know these women?

BERTRAM.

My lord, I neither can nor will deny

But that I know them. Do they charge me further?

DIANA.

Why do you look so strange upon your wife?

BERTRAM.

She's none of mine, my lord.

DIANA.

If you shall marry,

You give away this hand, and that is mine,

You give away heaven's vows, and those are mine,

You give away myself, which is known mine;

For I by vow am so embodied yours

That she which marries you must marry me,

Either both or none.

LAFEW.

[To Bertram] Your reputation comes too short for my daughter; you are no husband for her.

BERTRAM.

My lord, this is a fond and desperate creature

Whom sometime I have laugh'd with. Let your highness

Lay a more noble thought upon mine honour

Than for to think that I would sink it here.

KING.

Sir, for my thoughts, you have them ill to friend

Till your deeds gain them; fairer prove your honour

Than in my thought it lies!

DIANA.

Good my lord,

Ask him upon his oath, if he does think

He had not my virginity.

KING.

What say'st thou to her?

BERTRAM.

She's impudent, my lord,

And was a common gamester to the camp.

DIANA.

He does me wrong, my lord; if I were so

He might have bought me at a common price.

Do not believe him. O, behold this ring,

Whose high respect and rich validity

Did lack a parallel; yet for all that

He gave it to a commoner o' the camp,

If I be one.

COUNTESS.

He blushes, and 'tis it.

Of six preceding ancestors, that gem

Conferr'd by testament to th' sequent issue,

Hath it been owed and worn. This is his wife;

That ring's a thousand proofs.

KING.

Methought you said

You saw one here in court could witness it.

DIANA.

I did, my lord, but loath am to produce

So bad an instrument; his name's Parolles.

LAFEW.

I saw the man today, if man he be.

KING.

Find him, and bring him hither.

[Exit an Attendant.]

BERTRAM.

What of him?

He's quoted for a most perfidious slave,

With all the spots o' the world tax'd and debauch'd:

Whose nature sickens but to speak a truth.

Am I or that or this for what he'll utter,

That will speak anything?

KING.

She hath that ring of yours.

BERTRAM.

I think she has. Certain it is I lik'd her

And boarded her i' the wanton way of youth.

She knew her distance, and did angle for me,

Madding my eagerness with her restraint,

As all impediments in fancy's course

Are motives of more fancy; and in fine,

Her infinite cunning with her modern grace,

Subdu'd me to her rate; she got the ring,

And I had that which any inferior might

At market-price have bought.

DIANA.

I must be patient.

You that have turn'd off a first so noble wife

May justly diet me. I pray you yet,—

Since you lack virtue, I will lose a husband—

Send for your ring, I will return it home,

And give me mine again.

BERTRAM.

I have it not.

KING.

What ring was yours, I pray you?

DIANA.

Sir, much like

The same upon your finger.

KING.

Know you this ring? This ring was his of late.

DIANA.

And this was it I gave him, being abed.

KING.

The story then goes false you threw it him

Out of a casement.

DIANA.

I have spoke the truth.

Enter Attendant with Parolles.

BERTRAM.

My lord, I do confess the ring was hers.

KING.

You boggle shrewdly; every feather starts you.

Is this the man you speak of?

DIANA.

Ay, my lord.

KING.

Tell me, sirrah, but tell me true I charge you,

Not fearing the displeasure of your master,

Which on your just proceeding, I'll keep off,—

By him and by this woman here what know you?

PAROLLES.

So please your majesty, my master hath been an honourable gentleman.
Tricks he hath had in him, which gentlemen have.

KING.

Come, come, to the purpose. Did he love this woman?

PAROLLES.

Faith, sir, he did love her; but how?

KING.

How, I pray you?

PAROLLES.

He did love her, sir, as a gentleman loves a woman.

KING.

How is that?

PAROLLES.

He lov'd her, sir, and lov'd her not.

KING.

As thou art a knave and no knave.

What an equivocal companion is this!

PAROLLES.

I am a poor man, and at your majesty's command.

LAFEW.

He's a good drum, my lord, but a naughty orator.

DIANA.

Do you know he promised me marriage?

PAROLLES.

Faith, I know more than I'll speak.

KING.

But wilt thou not speak all thou know'st?

PAROLLES.

Yes, so please your majesty. I did go between them as I said; but more than that, he loved her, for indeed he was mad for her, and talked of Satan, and of Limbo, and of furies, and I know not what: yet I was in that credit with them at that time that I knew of their going to bed; and of other motions, as promising her marriage, and things which would derive me ill will to speak of; therefore I will not speak what I know.

KING.

Thou hast spoken all already, unless thou canst say they are married; but thou art too fine in thy evidence; therefore stand aside. This ring, you say, was yours?

DIANA.

Ay, my good lord.

KING.

Where did you buy it? Or who gave it you?

DIANA.

It was not given me, nor I did not buy it.

KING.

Who lent it you?

DIANA.

It was not lent me neither.

KING.

Where did you find it then?

DIANA.

I found it not.

KING.

If it were yours by none of all these ways,

How could you give it him?

DIANA.

I never gave it him.

LAFEW.

This woman's an easy glove, my lord; she goes off and on at pleasure.

KING.

This ring was mine, I gave it his first wife.

DIANA.

It might be yours or hers for ought I know.

KING.

Take her away, I do not like her now.

To prison with her. And away with him.

Unless thou tell'st me where thou hadst this ring,

Thou diest within this hour.

DIANA.

I'll never tell you.

KING.

Take her away.

DIANA.

I'll put in bail, my liege.

KING.

I think thee now some common customer.

DIANA.

By Jove, if ever I knew man, 'twas you.

KING.

Wherefore hast thou accus'd him all this while?

DIANA.

Because he's guilty, and he is not guilty.

He knows I am no maid, and he'll swear to't:

I'll swear I am a maid, and he knows not.

Great King, I am no strumpet, by my life;

I am either maid, or else this old man's wife.

[Pointing to Lafew.]

KING.

She does abuse our ears; to prison with her.

DIANA.

Good mother, fetch my bail. Stay, royal sir;

[Exit Widow.]

The jeweller that owes the ring is sent for,

And he shall surety me. But for this lord

Who hath abus'd me as he knows himself,

Though yet he never harm'd me, here I quit him.

He knows himself my bed he hath defil'd;

And at that time he got his wife with child.

Dead though she be, she feels her young one kick;

So there's my riddle: one that's dead is quick,

And now behold the meaning.

Enter Widow with Helena.

KING.

Is there no exorcist

Beguiles the truer office of mine eyes?

Is't real that I see?

HELENA.

No, my good lord;

'Tis but the shadow of a wife you see,

The name, and not the thing.

BERTRAM.

Both, both. O, pardon!

HELENA.

O, my good lord, when I was like this maid;

I found you wondrous kind. There is your ring,

And, look you, here's your letter. This it says,

'When from my finger you can get this ring,

And is by me with child, &c.' This is done;

Will you be mine now you are doubly won?

BERTRAM.

If she, my liege, can make me know this clearly,

I'll love her dearly, ever, ever dearly.

HELENA.

If it appear not plain, and prove untrue,

Deadly divorce step between me and you!

O my dear mother, do I see you living?

LAFEW.

Mine eyes smell onions; I shall weep anon.

[to Parolles] Good Tom Drum, lend me a handkercher.

So, I thank thee. Wait on me home, I'll make sport with thee.

Let thy courtesies alone, they are scurvy ones.

KING.

Let us from point to point this story know,

To make the even truth in pleasure flow.

[To Diana.] If thou beest yet a fresh uncropped flower,

Choose thou thy husband, and I'll pay thy dower;

For I can guess that by thy honest aid,

Thou kept'st a wife herself, thyself a maid.

Of that and all the progress more and less,

Resolvedly more leisure shall express.

All yet seems well, and if it end so meet,

The bitter past, more welcome is the sweet.

[Flourish.]

[EPILOGUE]

The king's a beggar, now the play is done;

All is well ended if this suit be won,

That you express content; which we will pay

With strife to please you, day exceeding day.

Ours be your patience then, and yours our parts;

Your gentle hands lend us, and take our hearts.

[Exeunt omnes.]

About Author

Shakespeare produced most of his known works between 1589 and 1613. His early plays were primarily comedies and histories and are regarded as some of the best work produced in these genres. Until about 1608, he wrote mainly tragedies, among them Hamlet, Othello, King Lear, and Macbeth, all considered to be among the finest works in the English language. In the last phase of his life, he wrote tragicomedies (also known as romances) and collaborated with other playwrights.

Many of Shakespeare's plays were published in editions of varying quality and accuracy in his lifetime. However, in 1623, two fellow actors and friends of Shakespeare's, John Heminges and Henry Condell, published a more definitive text known as the First Folio, a posthumous collected edition of Shakespeare's dramatic works that included all but two of his plays. The volume was prefaced with a poem by Ben Jonson, in which Jonson presciently hails Shakespeare in a now-famous quote as "not of an age, but for all time".

Throughout the 20th and 21st centuries, Shakespeare's works have been continually adapted and rediscovered by new movements in scholarship and performance. His plays remain popular and are studied, performed, and reinterpreted through various cultural and political contexts around the world.

Early life

William Shakespeare was the son of John Shakespeare, an alderman and a successful glover (glove-maker) originally from Snitterfield, and Mary Arden, the daughter of an affluent landowning farmer. He was born in Stratford-upon-Avon and baptised there on 26 April 1564. His actual date of birth remains unknown, but is traditionally observed on 23 April, Saint George's Day. This date, which can be traced to a mistake made by an 18th-century scholar, has proved appealing to biographers because Shakespeare died on the same date in 1616. He was the third of eight children, and the eldest surviving son.

Although no attendance records for the period survive, most biographers agree that Shakespeare was probably educated at the King's New School in Stratford, a free school chartered in 1553, about a quarter-mile (400 m) from his home. Grammar schools varied in quality during the Elizabethan era, but grammar school curricula were largely similar: the basic Latin text was standardised by royal decree, and the school would have provided an intensive education in grammar based upon Latin classical authors.

At the age of 18, Shakespeare married 26-year-old Anne Hathaway. The consistory court of the Diocese of Worcester issued a marriage licence on 27 November 1582. The next day, two of Hathaway's neighbours posted bonds guaranteeing that no lawful claims impeded the marriage. The ceremony may have been arranged in some haste since the Worcester chancellor allowed the marriage banns to be read once instead of the usual three times, and six months after the marriage Anne gave birth to a daughter, Susanna, baptised 26 May 1583. Twins, son Hamnet and daughter Judith, followed almost two years later and were baptised 2 February 1585. Hamnet died of unknown causes at the age of 11 and was buried 11 August 1596.

After the birth of the twins, Shakespeare left few historical traces until he is mentioned as part of the London theatre scene in 1592. The exception is the appearance of his name in the "complaints bill" of a law case before the Queen's Bench court at Westminster dated Michaelmas Term 1588 and 9 October 1589. Scholars refer to the years between 1585 and 1592 as Shakespeare's "lost years". Biographers attempting to account for this period have reported many apocryphal stories. Nicholas Rowe, Shakespeare's first biographer, recounted a Stratford legend that Shakespeare fled the town for London to escape prosecution for deer poaching in the estate of local squire Thomas Lucy. Shakespeare is also supposed to have taken his revenge on Lucy by writing a scurrilous ballad about him. Another 18th-century story has Shakespeare starting his theatrical career minding the horses of theatre patrons in London. John Aubrey reported that Shakespeare had been a country schoolmaster. Some 20th-century scholars have suggested that Shakespeare may have been employed as a schoolmaster by Alexander

Hoghton of Lancashire, a Catholic landowner who named a certain "William Shakeshafte" in his will. Little evidence substantiates such stories other than hearsay collected after his death, and Shakeshafte was a common name in the Lancashire area.

London and theatrical career

It is not known definitively when Shakespeare began writing, but contemporary allusions and records of performances show that several of his plays were on the London stage by 1592. By then, he was sufficiently known in London to be attacked in print by the playwright Robert Greene in his Groats-Worth of Wit:

... there is an upstart Crow, beautified with our feathers, that with his Tiger's heart wrapped in a Player's hide, supposes he is as well able to bombast out a blank verse as the best of you: and being an absolute Johannes factotum, is in his own conceit the only Shake-scene in a country.

Scholars differ on the exact meaning of Greene's words, but most agree that Greene was accusing Shakespeare of reaching above his rank in trying to match such university-educated writers as Christopher Marlowe, Thomas Nashe, and Greene himself (the so-called "University Wits"). The italicised phrase parodying the line "Oh, tiger's heart wrapped in a woman's hide" from Shakespeare's Henry VI, Part 3, along with the pun "Shake-scene", clearly identify Shakespeare as Greene's target. As used here, Johannes Factotum ("Jack of all trades") refers to a second-rate tinkerer with the work of others, rather than the more common "universal genius".

Greene's attack is the earliest surviving mention of Shakespeare's work in the theatre. Biographers suggest that his career may have begun any time from the mid-1580s to just before Greene's remarks. After 1594, Shakespeare's plays were performed only by the Lord Chamberlain's Men, a company owned by a group of players, including Shakespeare, that soon became the leading playing company in London. After the death of Queen Elizabeth in 1603, the company was awarded a royal patent by the new King James I, and changed its name to the King's Men.

"All the world's a stage,

and all the men and women merely players:

they have their exits and their entrances;

and one man in his time plays many parts ..."

—As You Like It, Act II, Scene 7, 139–142

In 1599, a partnership of members of the company built their own theatre on the south bank of the River Thames, which they named the Globe. In 1608, the partnership also took over the Blackfriars indoor theatre. Extant records of Shakespeare's property purchases and investments indicate that his association with the company made him a wealthy man, and in 1597, he bought the second-largest house in Stratford, New Place, and in 1605, invested in a share of the parish tithes in Stratford.

Some of Shakespeare's plays were published in quarto editions, beginning in 1594, and by 1598, his name had become a selling point and began to appear on the title pages. Shakespeare continued to act in his own and other plays after his success as a playwright. The 1616 edition of Ben Jonson's Works names him on the cast lists for Every Man in His Humour (1598) and Sejanus His Fall (1603). The absence of his name from the 1605 cast list for Jonson's Volpone is taken by some scholars as a sign that his acting career was nearing its end. The First Folio of 1623, however, lists Shakespeare as one of "the Principal Actors in all these Plays", some of which were first staged after Volpone, although we cannot know for certain which roles he played. In 1610, John Davies of Hereford wrote that "good Will" played "kingly" roles. In 1709, Rowe passed down a tradition that Shakespeare played the ghost of Hamlet's father. Later traditions maintain that he also played Adam in As You Like It, and the Chorus in Henry V, though scholars doubt the sources of that information.

Throughout his career, Shakespeare divided his time between London and Stratford. In 1596, the year before he bought New Place as his family home in Stratford, Shakespeare was living in the parish of St. Helen's, Bishopsgate, north of the River Thames. He moved across the river to Southwark by 1599, the same year his company constructed the Globe Theatre there. By 1604, he had moved north of the river again, to an area north of St Paul's Cathedral with many fine houses. There, he rented rooms from a French Huguenot named Christopher Mountjoy, a maker of ladies' wigs and other headgear.

Later years and death

Rowe was the first biographer to record the tradition, repeated by Johnson, that Shakespeare retired to Stratford "some years before his death". He was still working as an actor in London in 1608; in an answer to the sharers' petition in 1635, Cuthbert Burbage stated that after purchasing the lease of the Blackfriars Theatre in 1608 from Henry Evans, the King's Men "placed men players" there, "which were Heminges, Condell, Shakespeare, etc.". However, it is perhaps relevant that the bubonic plague raged in London throughout 1609. The London public playhouses were repeatedly closed during extended outbreaks of the plague (a total of over 60 months closure between May 1603 and February 1610), which meant there was often no acting work. Retirement from all work was uncommon at that time. Shakespeare continued to visit London during the years 1611–1614. In 1612, he was called as a witness in Bellott v. Mountjoy, a court case concerning the marriage settlement of Mountjoy's daughter, Mary. In March 1613, he bought a gatehouse in the former Blackfriars priory; and from November 1614, he was in London for several weeks with his son-in-law, John Hall. After 1610, Shakespeare wrote fewer plays, and none are attributed to him after 1613. His last three plays were collaborations, probably with John Fletcher, who succeeded him as the house playwright of the King's Men.

Shakespeare died on 23 April 1616, at the age of 52. He died within a month of signing his will, a document which he begins by describing himself as being in "perfect health". No extant contemporary source explains how or why he died. Half a century later, John Ward, the vicar of Stratford, wrote in his notebook: "Shakespeare, Drayton, and Ben Jonson had a merry meeting and, it seems, drank too hard, for Shakespeare died of a fever there contracted", not an impossible scenario since Shakespeare knew Jonson and Drayton. Of the tributes from fellow authors, one refers to his relatively sudden death: "We wondered, Shakespeare, that thou went'st so soon / From the world's stage to the grave's tiring room."

He was survived by his wife and two daughters. Susanna had married a physician, John Hall, in 1607, and Judith had married Thomas Quiney, a vintner, two months before Shakespeare's death. Shakespeare signed his last will and testament on 25 March 1616; the following day, his new son-in-law, Thomas Quiney was found guilty of fathering an illegitimate son by Margaret Wheeler, who had died during childbirth. Thomas was ordered by the church court to do public penance, which would have caused much shame and embarrassment for the Shakespeare family.

Shakespeare bequeathed the bulk of his large estate to his elder daughter Susanna under stipulations that she pass it down intact to "the first son of her body". The Quineys had three children, all of whom died without marrying. The Halls had one child, Elizabeth, who married twice but died without children in 1670, ending Shakespeare's direct line. Shakespeare's will scarcely mentions his wife, Anne, who was probably entitled to one-third of his estate automatically. He did make a point, however, of leaving her "my second best bed", a bequest that has led to much speculation. Some scholars see the bequest as an insult to Anne, whereas others believe that the second-best bed would have been the matrimonial bed and therefore rich in significance.

Shakespeare was buried in the chancel of the Holy Trinity Church two days after his death. The epitaph carved into the stone slab covering his grave includes a curse against moving his bones, which was carefully avoided during restoration of the church in 2008:

Good frend for Iesvs sake forbeare,

To digg the dvst encloased heare.

Bleste be Middle English the.svg man Middle English that.svg spares thes stones,

And cvrst be he Middle English that.svg moves my bones.

(Modern spelling: Good friend, for Jesus' sake forbear, / To dig the dust enclosed here. / Blessed be the man that spares these stones, / And cursed be he that moves my bones.)

Some time before 1623, a funerary monument was erected in his memory on the north wall, with a half-effigy of him in the act of writing. Its plaque compares him to Nestor, Socrates, and Virgil. In 1623, in conjunction with the publication of the First Folio, the Droeshout engraving was published.

Shakespeare has been commemorated in many statues and memorials around the world, including funeral monuments in Southwark Cathedral and Poets' Corner in Westminster Abbey.

Plays

Most playwrights of the period typically collaborated with others at some point, and critics agree that Shakespeare did the same, mostly early and late in his career. Some attributions, such as Titus Andronicus and the early history plays, remain controversial while The Two Noble Kinsmen and the lost Cardenio have well-attested contemporary documentation. Textual evidence also supports the view that several of the plays were revised by other writers after their original composition.

The first recorded works of Shakespeare are Richard III and the three parts of Henry VI, written in the early 1590s during a vogue for historical drama. Shakespeare's plays are difficult to date precisely, however, and studies of the texts suggest that Titus Andronicus, The Comedy of Errors, The Taming of the Shrew, and The Two Gentlemen of Verona may also belong to Shakespeare's earliest period. His first histories, which draw heavily on the 1587 edition of Raphael Holinshed's Chronicles of England, Scotland, and Ireland, dramatise the destructive results of weak or corrupt rule and have been interpreted as a justification for the origins of the Tudor dynasty. The early plays were influenced by the works of other Elizabethan dramatists, especially Thomas Kyd and Christopher Marlowe, by the traditions of medieval drama, and by the plays of Seneca. The Comedy of Errors was also based on classical models, but no source for The Taming of the Shrew has been found, though it is related to a separate play of the same name and may have derived from a folk story. Like The Two Gentlemen of Verona, in which two friends appear to approve of rape, the Shrew's story of the taming of a woman's independent spirit by a man sometimes troubles modern critics, directors, and audiences.

Shakespeare's early classical and Italianate comedies, containing tight double plots and precise comic sequences, give way in the mid-1590s to the romantic atmosphere of his most acclaimed comedies. A Midsummer Night's Dream is a witty mixture of romance, fairy magic, and comic lowlife scenes. Shakespeare's next comedy, the equally romantic Merchant of Venice, contains a portrayal of the vengeful Jewish moneylender Shylock, which reflects Elizabethan views but may appear derogatory to modern audiences. The wit and wordplay of Much Ado About Nothing, the charming rural setting of As You Like It, and the lively merrymaking of Twelfth Night complete Shakespeare's sequence of great comedies. After the lyrical Richard II, written almost entirely in verse, Shakespeare introduced prose comedy into the histories of the late 1590s, Henry IV, parts 1 and 2, and Henry V. His characters become more complex and tender as he switches deftly between comic and serious scenes, prose and poetry, and achieves the narrative variety of his mature work. This period begins and ends with two tragedies: Romeo and Juliet, the famous romantic tragedy of sexually charged adolescence, love, and death; and Julius Caesar—based on Sir Thomas North's 1579 translation of Plutarch's Parallel Lives—which introduced a new kind of drama. According to Shakespearean scholar James Shapiro, in Julius Caesar, "the various strands of politics, character, inwardness, contemporary events, even Shakespeare's own reflections on the act of writing, began to infuse each other".

In the early 17th century, Shakespeare wrote the so-called "problem plays" Measure for Measure, Troilus and Cressida, and All's Well That Ends Well and a number of his best known tragedies. Many critics believe that Shakespeare's greatest tragedies represent the peak of his art. The titular hero of one of Shakespeare's greatest tragedies, Hamlet, has probably been discussed more than any other Shakespearean character, especially for his famous soliloquy which begins "To be or not to be; that is the question". Unlike the introverted Hamlet, whose fatal flaw is hesitation, the heroes of the tragedies that followed, Othello and King Lear, are undone by hasty errors of judgement. The plots of Shakespeare's tragedies often hinge on such fatal errors or flaws, which overturn order and destroy the hero and those he loves. In Othello, the villain Iago stokes Othello's sexual jealousy to the point where he murders the innocent wife who loves him. In King Lear, the old king commits the tragic error of giving up his powers, initiating the events which lead to the torture and blinding of the Earl of Gloucester and the murder of Lear's youngest daughter Cordelia. According to the critic Frank Kermode, "the play-offers neither its good characters nor its audience any relief from its cruelty". In Macbeth, the shortest and most compressed of Shakespeare's tragedies, uncontrollable ambition incites Macbeth and his wife, Lady Macbeth, to murder the rightful king and usurp the throne until their own guilt destroys them in turn. In this play, Shakespeare adds a supernatural element to the tragic structure. His last major tragedies, Antony and Cleopatra and Coriolanus, contain some of Shakespeare's finest poetry and were considered his most successful tragedies by the poet and critic T.S. Eliot.

In his final period, Shakespeare turned to romance or tragicomedy and completed three more major plays: Cymbeline, The Winter's Tale, and The Tempest, as well as the collaboration, Pericles, Prince of Tyre. Less bleak than the tragedies, these four plays are graver in tone than the comedies of the 1590s, but they end with reconciliation and the forgiveness of potentially tragic errors. Some commentators have seen this change in mood as evidence of a more serene view of life on Shakespeare's part, but it may merely reflect the theatrical fashion of the day. Shakespeare collaborated on two further surviving plays, Henry VIII and The Two Noble Kinsmen, probably with John Fletcher.

Performances

It is not clear for which companies Shakespeare wrote his early plays. The title page of the 1594 edition of Titus Andronicus reveals that the play had been acted by three different troupes. After the plagues of 1592–3, Shakespeare's plays were performed by his own company at The Theatre and the Curtain in Shoreditch, north of the Thames. Londoners flocked there to see the first part of Henry IV, Leonard Digges recording, "Let but Falstaff come, Hal, Poins, the rest ... and you scarce shall have a room". When the company found themselves in dispute with their landlord, they pulled The

Theatre down and used the timbers to construct the Globe Theatre, the first playhouse built by actors for actors, on the south bank of the Thames at Southwark. The Globe opened in autumn 1599, with Julius Caesar one of the first plays staged. Most of Shakespeare's greatest post-1599 plays were written for the Globe, including Hamlet, Othello, and King Lear.

After the Lord Chamberlain's Men were renamed the King's Men in 1603, they entered a special relationship with the new King James. Although the performance records are patchy, the King's Men performed seven of Shakespeare's plays at court between 1 November 1604, and 31 October 1605, including two performances of The Merchant of Venice. After 1608, they performed at the indoor Blackfriars Theatre during the winter and the Globe during the summer. The indoor setting, combined with the Jacobean fashion for lavishly staged masques, allowed Shakespeare to introduce more elaborate stage devices. In Cymbeline, for example, Jupiter descends "in thunder and lightning, sitting upon an eagle: he throws a thunderbolt. The ghosts fall on their knees."

The actors in Shakespeare's company included the famous Richard Burbage, William Kempe, Henry Condell and John Heminges. Burbage played the leading role in the first performances of many of Shakespeare's plays, including Richard III, Hamlet, Othello, and King Lear. The popular comic actor Will Kempe played the servant Peter in Romeo and Juliet and Dogberry in Much Ado About Nothing, among other characters. He was replaced around 1600 by Robert Armin, who played roles such as Touchstone in As You Like It and the fool in King Lear. In 1613, Sir Henry Wotton recorded that Henry VIII "was set forth with many extraordinary circumstances of pomp and ceremony". On 29 June, however, a cannon set fire to the thatch of the Globe and burned the theatre to the ground, an event which pinpoints the date of a Shakespeare play with rare precision.

Textual sources

In 1623, John Heminges and Henry Condell, two of Shakespeare's friends from the King's Men, published the First Folio, a collected edition of Shakespeare's plays. It contained 36 texts, including 18 printed for the first time. Many of the plays had already appeared in quarto versions— flimsy books made from sheets of paper folded twice to make four leaves. No evidence suggests that Shakespeare approved these editions, which the First Folio describes as "stol'n and surreptitious copies". Nor did Shakespeare plan or expect his works to survive in any form at all; those works likely would have faded into oblivion but for his friends' spontaneous idea, after his death, to create and publish the First Folio.

Alfred Pollard termed some of the pre-1623 versions as "bad quartos" because of their adapted, paraphrased or garbled texts, which may in places have been reconstructed from memory. Where several versions of a play survive, each differs from the other. The differences may stem from copying or printing errors, from notes by actors or audience members, or from Shakespeare's own papers. In some cases, for example, Hamlet, Troilus and Cressida, and Othello, Shakespeare could have revised the texts between the quarto and folio editions. In the case of King Lear, however, while most modern editions do conflate them, the 1623 folio version is so different from the 1608 quarto that the Oxford Shakespeare prints them both, arguing that they cannot be conflated without confusion.

Influence from neighbours in London

Ten years of research by Geoffrey Marsh (museum director) of the Victoria and Albert Museum in London may have shown that Shakespeare got many of the ideas and information for his plays, from his neighbours that he lived near in London in the late 1590s.

Geoffrey Marsh found the site of Shakespeare's house in St Helen's Church, Bishopsgate parish, at the corner of St.Helen's churchyard and Bishopsgate Street, north of the churchyard, from the records of the Leathersellers Company. Many wealthy and notable people (including Sir John Spencer and Dr. Edward Jorden and Dr. Peter Turner), with connections across Europe, lived near Shakespeare.

Poems

In 1593 and 1594, when the theatres were closed because of plague,

Shakespeare published two narrative poems on sexual themes, Venus and Adonis and The Rape of Lucrece. He dedicated them to Henry Wriothesley, Earl of Southampton. In Venus and Adonis, an innocent Adonis rejects the sexual advances of Venus; while in The Rape of Lucrece, the virtuous wife Lucrece is raped by the lustful Tarquin. Influenced by Ovid's Metamorphoses, the poems show the guilt and moral confusion that result from uncontrolled lust. Both proved popular and were often reprinted during Shakespeare's lifetime. A third narrative poem, A Lover's Complaint, in which a young woman laments her seduction by a persuasive suitor, was printed in the first edition of the Sonnets in 1609. Most scholars now accept that Shakespeare wrote A Lover's Complaint. Critics consider that its fine qualities are marred by leaden effects. The Phoenix and the Turtle, printed in Robert Chester's 1601 Love's Martyr, mourns the deaths of the legendary phoenix and his lover, the faithful turtle dove. In 1599, two early drafts of sonnets 138 and 144 appeared in The Passionate Pilgrim, published under Shakespeare's name but without his permission.

Sonnets

Published in 1609, the Sonnets were the last of Shakespeare's non-dramatic works to be printed. Scholars are not certain when each of the 154 sonnets was composed, but evidence suggests that Shakespeare wrote sonnets throughout his career for a private readership. Even before the two unauthorised sonnets appeared in The Passionate Pilgrim in 1599, Francis Meres had referred in 1598 to Shakespeare's "sugred Sonnets among his private friends". Few analysts believe that the published collection follows Shakespeare's intended sequence. He seems to have planned two contrasting series: one about uncontrollable lust for a married woman of dark complexion (the "dark lady"), and one about conflicted love for a fair young man (the "fair youth"). It remains unclear if these figures represent real individuals, or if the authorial "I" who addresses them represents Shakespeare himself, though Wordsworth believed that with the sonnets "Shakespeare unlocked his heart".

"Shall I compare thee to a summer's day?

Thou art more lovely and more temperate ..."

—Lines from Shakespeare's Sonnet 18.

The 1609 edition was dedicated to a "Mr. W.H.", credited as "the only begetter" of the poems. It is not known whether this was written by Shakespeare himself or by the publisher, Thomas Thorpe, whose initials appear at the foot of the dedication page; nor is it known who Mr. W.H. was, despite numerous theories, or whether Shakespeare even authorised the publication. Critics praise the Sonnets as a profound meditation on the nature of love, sexual passion, procreation, death, and time.

Style

Shakespeare's first plays were written in the conventional style of the day. He wrote them in a stylised language that does not always spring naturally from the needs of the characters or the drama. The poetry depends on extended, sometimes elaborate metaphors and conceits, and the language is often rhetorical—written for actors to declaim rather than speak. The grand speeches in Titus Andronicus, in the view of some critics, often hold up the action, for example; and the verse in The Two Gentlemen of Verona has been described as stilted.

However, Shakespeare soon began to adapt the traditional styles to his own purposes. The opening soliloquy of Richard III has its roots in the self-declaration of Vice in medieval drama. At the same time, Richard's vivid self-awareness looks forward to the soliloquies of Shakespeare's mature plays. No single play marks a change from the traditional to the freer style. Shakespeare combined the two throughout his career, with Romeo and Juliet perhaps the best example of the mixing of the styles. By the time of Romeo and Juliet, Richard II, and A Midsummer Night's Dream in the mid-1590s, Shakespeare had begun to write a more natural poetry. He increasingly tuned his metaphors and images to the needs of the drama itself.

Shakespeare's standard poetic form was blank verse, composed in iambic pentameter. In practice, this meant that his verse was usually unrhymed and consisted of ten syllables to a line, spoken with a stress on every second syllable. The blank verse of his early plays is quite different from that of his later ones. It is often beautiful, but its sentences tend to start, pause, and finish at the end of lines, with the risk of monotony. Once Shakespeare mastered traditional blank verse, he began to interrupt and vary its flow. This technique releases the new power and flexibility of the poetry in plays such as Julius Caesar and Hamlet. Shakespeare uses it, for example, to convey the turmoil in Hamlet's mind:

> Sir, in my heart there was a kind of fighting
>
> That would not let me sleep. Methought I lay
>
> Worse than the mutines in the bilboes. Rashly—
>
> And prais'd be rashness for it—let us know
>
> Our indiscretion sometimes serves us well ...
>
> —Hamlet, Act 5, Scene 2, 4–8

After Hamlet, Shakespeare varied his poetic style further, particularly in the more emotional passages of the late tragedies. The literary critic A. C. Bradley described this style as "more concentrated, rapid, varied, and, in construction, less regular, not seldom twisted or elliptical". In the last phase of his career, Shakespeare adopted many techniques to achieve these effects. These included run-on lines, irregular pauses and stops, and extreme variations in sentence structure and length. In Macbeth, for example, the language darts from one unrelated metaphor or simile to another: "was the hope drunk/ Wherein you dressed yourself?" (1.7.35–38); "... pity, like a naked new-born babe/ Striding the blast, or heaven's cherubim, hors'd/ Upon the sightless couriers of the air ..." (1.7.21–25). The listener is challenged to complete the sense. The late romances, with their shifts in time and surprising turns of plot, inspired a last poetic style in which long and short sentences are set against one another, clauses are piled up, subject and object are reversed, and words are omitted, creating an effect of spontaneity.

Shakespeare combined poetic genius with a practical sense of the theatre. Like all playwrights of the time, he dramatised stories from sources such as Plutarch and Holinshed. He reshaped each plot to create several centres of interest and to show as many sides of a narrative to the audience as possible. This strength of design ensures that a Shakespeare play can survive translation, cutting and wide interpretation without loss to its core drama. As Shakespeare's mastery grew, he gave his characters clearer and more varied motivations and distinctive patterns of speech. He preserved aspects of his earlier style in the later plays, however. In Shakespeare's late romances, he deliberately returned to a more artificial style, which emphasised the illusion of theatre.

Influence

Shakespeare's work has made a lasting impression on later theatre and literature. In particular, he expanded the dramatic potential of characterisation, plot, language, and genre. Until Romeo and Juliet, for example, romance had not been viewed as a worthy topic for tragedy. Soliloquies had been used mainly to convey information about characters or events, but Shakespeare used them to explore characters' minds. His work heavily influenced later poetry. The Romantic poets attempted to revive Shakespearean verse drama, though with little success. Critic George Steiner described all English verse dramas from Coleridge to Tennyson as "feeble variations on Shakespearean themes."

Shakespeare influenced novelists such as Thomas Hardy, William Faulkner, and Charles Dickens. The American novelist Herman Melville's soliloquies owe much to Shakespeare; his Captain Ahab in Moby-Dick is a classic tragic hero, inspired by King Lear. Scholars have identified 20,000 pieces of music linked to Shakespeare's works. These include three operas by Giuseppe Verdi, Macbeth, Otello and Falstaff, whose critical standing compares with that of the source plays. Shakespeare has also inspired many painters, including the Romantics and the Pre-Raphaelites. The Swiss Romantic artist Henry Fuseli, a friend of William Blake, even translated Macbeth into German. The psychoanalyst Sigmund Freud drew on Shakespearean psychology, in particular, that of Hamlet, for his theories of human nature.

In Shakespeare's day, English grammar, spelling, and pronunciation were less standardised than they are now, and his use of language helped shape modern English. Samuel Johnson quoted him more often than any other author in his A Dictionary of the English Language, the first serious work of its type. Expressions such as "with bated breath" (Merchant of Venice) and "a foregone conclusion" (Othello) have found their way into everyday English speech.

Works

Classification of the plays

Shakespeare's works include the 36 plays printed in the First Folio of 1623, listed according to their folio classification as comedies, histories, and tragedies. Two plays not included in the First Folio, The Two Noble Kinsmen and Pericles, Prince of Tyre, are now accepted as part of the canon, with today's scholars agreeing that Shakespeare made major contributions to the writing of both. No Shakespearean poems were included in the First Folio.

In the late 19th century, Edward Dowden classified four of the late comedies as romances, and though many scholars prefer to call them tragicomedies, Dowden's term is often used. In 1896, Frederick S. Boas coined the term "problem plays" to describe four plays: All's Well That Ends Well, Measure for Measure, Troilus and Cressida, and Hamlet. "Dramas as singular in theme and temper cannot be strictly called comedies or tragedies", he wrote. "We may, therefore, borrow a convenient phrase from the theatre of today and class them together as Shakespeare's problem plays." The term, much debated and sometimes applied to other plays, remains in use, though Hamlet is definitively classed as a tragedy. (Source: Wikipedia)

CPSIA information can be obtained
at www.ICGtesting.com
Printed in the USA
BVHW071915080919
557876BV00001B/371/P